MASSACHUSETTS
BREWERIES

MASSACHUSETTS BREWERIES

JOHN HOLL & APRIL DARCY

STACKPOLE
BOOKS

Published by
STACKPOLE BOOKS
5067 Ritter Road
Mechanicsburg, PA 17055
www.stackpolebooks.com

The authors and the publisher encourage readers to visit the breweries and
sample their beers, and recommend that those who consume alcoholic beverages travel with a designated nondrinking driver.

Printed in the United States of America

10 9 8 7 6 5 4 3 2 1

FIRST EDITION

Cover design by Tessa J. Sweigert
Labels and logos used with permission of the breweries
Author photo of April Darcy on back cover by Richard N. Alfonzo

Library of Congress Cataloging-in-Publication Data

Holl, John.
    Massachusetts breweries / John Holl & April Darcy. — 1st ed.
      p.   cm.
    Includes index.
    ISBN 978-0-8117-1052-7 (pbk.)
    1. Bars (Drinking establishments)—Massachusetts—Guidebooks.
2. Microbreweries—Massachusetts—Guidebooks. 3. Breweries—
Massachusetts—Guidebooks. I. Darcy, April. II. Title.
TX950.57.M5H65   2012
647.95744–dc23
                                         2012013861

Contents

Foreword

We were college freshmen when we met at the Father's Six in Harvard Square and formed a friendship initiated by our love of beer. Thus began our Massachusetts craft beer journey. To say the local beer landscape was bleak back in the early and mid-1980s would be an understatement. Imported yellow lagers were considered exciting, and while there were quite a few to choose from, it was nearly impossible to discern one from another; only the labels provided an individual personality and character. Traveling in Europe after college showed us how much we were missing at home. We figured, if we can't buy the beer we want to drink, then let's brew it ourselves. Here we are twenty-five years later, cofounders of the oldest and largest craft brewery in Massachusetts, writing the foreword of a book about Massachusetts beer! This topic would have been entirely historical all those years ago—a look back on a proud but vanished industry. Today, however, we can look around and see a vibrant community of brewers and beer lovers with the promise of a very bright future.

If you've ever driven in and around Boston and are unfamiliar with the lay of the land, you can attest to the fact that it can be difficult to navigate. When we first met John Holl, he had successfully found his way to our brewery on the South Boston waterfront, which before the addition of the Silver Line public transportation and several upscale restaurants next door was a feat unto itself. John had asked if he could join us for the monthly meeting of the newly formed Massachusetts Brewers Guild to discuss a new book he was writing about Massachusetts brewers. This was exciting news. After some lively discussion over a couple pints, we were content knowing that our stories would be told by someone with the same passion and appreciation for beer and beer culture that we all shared as a guild.

Each year hundreds of thousands of people visit Massachusetts. With its rich landscape of beer and breweries, the state is becoming a beer destination in its own right, with world-class breweries in every corner. John and his co-author, April Darcy, should be considered your Massachusetts beer navigators and this book your beer compass. Using it as your guide, you will be able to chart your course of beer exploration from the Berkshires to the Cape via the twisty streets of Boston.

Speaking of exploration, it should be noted that history suggests the Pilgrims landed in Massachusetts because they ran out of beer aboard the *Mayflower*. This was clearly a foreshadowing of the great beer state that was to come.

Today there are more than forty brewing licenses issued in the state, including brewpubs, farmer-breweries, and manufacturers. Harpoon was granted Brewing Permit #001 in 1986 by the Commonwealth of Massachusetts because we were the first to commercially brew and bottle beer in the state after a significant dormant period. At the time, there was one brewpub (now long closed) and a contract brewer, but no packaging breweries. In the beginning, our beer was a novelty. For the old-timers, it was reminiscent of the romance from old favorites that had gone away like Harvard in Lowell, Haffenreffer in Boston, Tadcaster in Worcester, and Hampden out in the Pioneer Valley. For younger beer drinkers there was excitement over something new. That sense of discovery along with deference to history and tradition is what we love about brewing beer in Massachusetts.

We feel fortunate to brew in Massachusetts not only because of our fellow brewers who make it interesting and fun, but because of the passionate drinkers who support local beer and make what we do possible. If there's one thing that can be said about the people of Massachusetts, it's that they do not withhold their opinions. If they don't like a beer, they'll let you know. Conversely, they'll be the first to tell you when they like something. It only makes us all better and work harder.

Back in the mid-1990s local brewing legends Ted and Jack Haffenreffer came to the brewery for a visit. They were both in their eighties, and they spent an afternoon here drinking beer and regaling us with great stories from brewing in Boston as far back as the 1920s and from before then as relayed to them by their father and grandfather. It was an amazing experience. We look forward to sharing our experiences with future generations of Massachusetts brewers. Until then we will continue to welcome beer lovers to our brewery, as was our goal when we started Harpoon. We are hopeful that this book will lead you to us for a beer and are confident that it will set you on your own exciting and flavorful Massachusetts beer journey. Happy beer travels!

—Rich Doyle and Dan Kenary
Cofounders, Harpoon Brewery

Acknowledgments

Although our names appear on the cover, it takes a larger group of people to publish a book. Throughout this process we have been assisted, encouraged, and inspired by many people. We've tested the patience of family, friends, and each other, but perhaps no one more than our intrepid editor Kyle Weaver. Not only is he skilled with a red pen, but he is also one of the kindest and most thoughtful people we have come to know in the publishing industry. He has our unyielding thanks, appreciation, and friendship. Also, we're grateful for the entire Stackpole team for their great support, especially Brett Keener, who expertly guided us in the production phase.

This book is based on previous guidebooks in the Stackpole series, pioneered by Lew Bryson. Always a gentleman, Lew has shared his wisdom and gave us hope when this book seemed like it would never be completed. Lew shared a piece of information a few years back that, while simple, has proved invaluable. We hope you will heed it as well: "Drink plenty of water, and never pass up an opportunity to urinate."

While traveling the state we were the recipients of hospitality and friendship from the following people: Katie Zezima, Dave Shaw, Kristen and Brian Holding, Andrea DeManbey, Liz Melby, Michelle Sullivan, Katie Piepora, Alex Somers, Patrick Alfonzo, Bill Toomey, Marc Cregan, Lee Chambers, Dan Kochakian, and Nancy Gardella.

We're grateful to our family and friends at home, especially our parents and siblings, for their continual support in all of our many writing and traveling endeavors. Many thanks go to Nate Schweber, Ted Romankow, Gina Golba, and Ray Schroth for their support, guidance, and friendship.

Massachusetts has long been a part of our lives, particularly for John, beginning even before his birth. Jim Knickman and Terry Clark, friends of John's parents, purchased a historic home in Harwich Port on Cape Cod, and ever since then, vibrant summers have been spent on the beach, on and in the water, and exploring both the salty and swanky nearby communities. Years later April would come to know and love the house as well, alongside all those who made so many original summer vacations memorable. This includes Annie Knickman;

Joe and Joanne DiSalvo and their children, Julia, Andrew, Katie, and Patrick; and of course John's parents, John and Mary, and brother Thomas. The house is filled with many fond memories, as well as a growing collection of Cape Cod Beer growlers that wait patiently to be filled during each visit.

Finally we're indebted to the owners, brewers, and staff of the places we visited and chronicled. Their support and enthusiasm made this project a happy one. We are honored to tell their stories.

Introduction

"We could not now take time for further search . . . our victuals being much spent, especially our beer." Those words are from a journal entry written by a passenger aboard the *Mayflower* in 1620. Had it not been for the low supply of brew aboard that famed ship destined for the New World, the Pilgrims might have continued with the original plan, which called for a landing in what is now Virginia. Instead they landed at Plymouth Rock and got down to the business of establishing a new life, and finding a way to brew.

This makes the bond between Massachusetts and beer a particularly strong one. It began a proud tradition of fine beers created by historic breweries over many years. In the last twenty-five or so years, Massachusetts has been an important place in the rebirth of local American breweries.

History of Brewing in the United States

By the time George Washington was elected president of our new nation, cider was the preferred fermented beverage. Imported beers from the Old World, mostly ales, were available. Rum was popular as well. But the young country was far from the beer-consuming nation it is today.

In the mid-1840s German immigrants arriving in the United States brought with them centuries of brewing tradition and know-how. Breweries began popping up in cities from Philadelphia to Milwaukee. Lager was the clear favorite for both brewers to produce and customers to consume. Beer became so popular and demand so great that by 1900 there were roughly two thousand breweries in the country.

Businesses like Anheuser-Busch of St. Louis and Best's Brewing Company of Milwaukee, which would later become Pabst, grew large while others remained small and some simply fell by the wayside.

All this drinking, however, upset some folks during the temperance movement of the late nineteenth century and early twentieth century, an organized effort to encourage abstinence from alcohol consumption. By 1920, they were able to push through a plan that would become a thirteen-year nightmare called Prohibition. Some brewers were able to stay afloat by selling sodas or near-beer, low-alcohol alternatives that compromised on ingredients and seriously damaged flavors. By the time Prohibition was repealed in 1933, few breweries were left standing. In fact, by the 1960s, there were only about forty breweries left in the country. Most of these were large and controlled the majority of the market, but a scattered few regional breweries survived. Mostly, however, what was on the shelves and on tap were lagers from the big breweries like Anheuser-Busch, a far cry from the brewing heyday just seven decades earlier.

Modern-Day Craft

With only a handful of breweries left in the United States, options were slim for anyone looking for a beer beyond the pale remains of once-proud lagers brewed in the Northeast and Midwest. One of the breweries that had survived was Anchor Brewing of San Francisco, but the financial books were in nearly as bad shape as the structure itself. Enter Fritz Maytag, of the appliance manufacturing family, who enjoyed the flavorful ales produced there and so used some of his fortune to purchase and rehab the brewery in the 1960s. He brought it back from the brink and turned it into one of the great American craft breweries. Maytag actually held onto the brewery until 2010, when he sold it to a group of investors.

But Anchor was already a modest-sized brewery when Maytag took over. It would take a scrappy, determined, and, some might say, crazy individual to start a brewery from scratch. That person wound up being Jack McAuliffe, who launched the New Albion Brewing Company in Sonoma, California, in 1976. What today would seem like an ordinary act of entrepreneurism was revolutionary back then. But to open a brewery, like McAuliffe did, with an annual capacity of just 450 barrels a year was unheard of, given that many of the existing breweries were producing many millions of barrels.

Furthermore, the equipment needed to brew such a small amount was extremely hard to come by. So, using his engineering background, McAuliffe got down to work, salvaged old dairy equipment, and welded together the rest to create a working brewery.

The beer was a hit, at least around Sonoma and California's Bay Area, and people would travel long distances to try this new "micro beer." The demand was there, but ultimately the funding was not. When McAuliffe needed capital to keep the brewery afloat, banks were reluctant to give him a loan. They looked at him, McAuliffe would later recall, like he was from Mars. So, just five years after opening New Albion, McAuliffe was forced to close. His equipment went north to

Mendocino Brewing, one of many that would open in his wake, and McAuliffe quit the brewing business altogether, moving around the country and eventually settling in Texas.

To this day, he claims he was not a pioneer and refuses to acknowledge any potential impact his brewery had on the American craft beer movement. But for those who knew McAuliffe and were inspired by him, his impact was undeniable. Ken Grossman, who was running a homebrew supply shop in Chico, California, around the time McAuliffe opened New Albion, visited the small brewery and realized that he too could open his own place. Today, Sierra Nevada Brewing Company is the second-largest craft brewery in America, according to the Brewer's Association, a trade group that monitors the craft beer industry. Samuel Adams is the largest, although the Massachusetts-based brewery creates most of its output in Pennsylvania and Ohio.

McAuliffe, Grossman, and others who opened in the late 1970s and early 1980s largely had homebrewers to thank. When homebrewing became legal, many of those who had already been doing it tried their hand at going pro. Those who didn't make the leap supported their local breweries and spurred them on, enhancing the bottom line and bringing new people to the fold. Homebrewers are a fervent lot and they continue to inspire and, in many cases, become the craft brewers that we know today and will be supporting tomorrow.

There have been peaks and valleys since McAuliffe first opened his brewery. The mid-1990s saw a glut of new breweries, some carrying borderline offensive names of animals and various bodily functions. Several of these breweries, playing off the public's newfound interest in craft, were good for a consumer laugh, but the product inside the bottles was lacking and a once-bitten consumer was too shy to go back.

Those that survived generally thrived. This second generation of brewers did things right, correctly marketing their brands, going for extreme beers with high alcohol content and strong hop flavor, playing into a niche of beer drinkers—younger mostly—who wanted to break away from their parents' beers. Some examples include Delaware's Dogfish Head Brewery and Pennsylvania's Victory Brewing.

Breweries opened and closed, others changed ownership, but things in the craft mostly stayed static for a while as people settled into a world with craft beer. Then, at the late part of the last decade, the brewing world began to see things ramp up again. A lot of this, strangely enough, can be attributed to the recession of the late 2000s. Many avid homebrewers got laid off from their full-time jobs and took it as a greater sign that it was time to follow their dreams and open a brewery. Funding, still easier to secure than it was for McAuliffe, could be obtained. Today it seems there are breweries opening in every town. The Brewer's Association recently put out a figure that said the majority of Americans now live within ten miles of a brewery. That's not tough to imagine when you consider that in the craft arena alone, there are more than nineteen hundred microbreweries and brewpubs in the United States. That's the highest number since Prohibition ended in 1933.

Massachusetts, as you will see, has a strong number of breweries, nearly fifty, and continues to add more to its ranks. This can only mean good things for thirsty residents and travelers to the state. But it has been a long road for Massachusetts and its breweries. To appreciate where we are today in Massachusetts, we will first take a brief look back.

History of Beer in Massachusetts

After the Pilgrims set up their colony in the early seventeenth century and others followed them to the New World, these pioneers got down to the business of setting up a new life and recreating many of the comforts of their old home. Predictably this involved taverns. The first tavern in Massachusetts was established in Boston when Samuel Cole opened his doors in 1633. Three years later, a Captain Sedgwick opened what is referred to as the commonwealth's first brewery; however, many tavern owners had the right to brew before that, and likely did. Brewing at home was also popular at the time, a chore often done by women. In 1640, the colony passed a regulation stating that a person should not be "allowed to brew beer unless he is a good brewer."

Move ahead to the American Revolution and the brewing tradition continued, with names that endure to this day. One, of course, is Samuel Adams, the famous patriot and signer of the Declaration of Independence. Adams was the son of a brewer-maltster, and he held the same job for a time before becoming involved in the politics of the era. He participated in many of the key events that led to a new government being formed and later served as governor of the commonwealth from 1794 to 1797. His name not only lives on in the annals of the nation, but also in the beer industry, courtesy of the Boston Beer Company.

The 1800s and early 1900s would see breweries open up and supply beer at a healthy rate. Most were centered in Boston, in the Jamaica Plain and Roxbury neighborhoods. This was spurred on by the fresh water supply found in those areas. One historical brewery of note was operated by John Roessle, who is credited as the "first" to brew lager in the commonwealth.

Prohibition, from 1920 to 1933, nearly killed off the forty or so breweries operating before its enactment, and the five that made it out the other side didn't last. It would be many decades before a new brewery would open. Harpoon, in Boston, has brewery license number 1 from this modern generation of brewers.

Other breweries have come and gone over the last twenty-five or so years, but the commitment that today's brewers have brought to their craft is a testament to history and the unyielding love so many have for this wonderful fermented beverage.

Brewpubs vs. Microbreweries

Massachusetts has a few large breweries, but none that come close to behemoth status. Instead, the commonwealth is filled with smaller *microbreweries*. They typically produce fewer than six million barrels annually (a barrel contains about thirty-one gallons) and serve a smaller geographical area. The largest in-state producer is Harpoon Brewery, which rolls out about 150,000 barrels per year. The commercial breweries typically bottle or can their beer and are able fill keg orders for bars and other customers. There are a number of contract breweries in the state that not only brew their house brands, but also fill orders for brewers who supply their own recipes but do not have the necessary equipment to meet orders and demand.

A *brewpub*, by comparison, is essentially a restaurant that has brewing equipment. There are exceptions, but in most cases, their beer is usually available on premises only and not sold in stores. Customers, however, can usually purchase half-gallon jugs, called *growlers*, to enjoy the beer at home.

The term *craft brewery* is also used a lot and can be interchangeable with the words brewpub and microbrewery. Simply put, the places mentioned in this book use quality ingredients, proper brewing methods, and embody a spirit reminiscent of earlier brewing pioneers.

"Every time I turn around it seems someone new is opening up," said Dan Kochakian, who covers Massachusetts for the *Ale Street News* and is one of the more welcoming and affable guys in the state's beer scene. "It's exciting. Everyone is experimenting."

Locally Grown

The experimentation continues with not only recipes, but also with ingredients. When the brewing scene suffered after Prohibition, many of the small businesses that supported the industry also took a hit. This included hop growers and maltsters. As it grew, craft beer had to rely on the major ingredients producers that also service the larger clients. However, there has been a shift in recent years and now smaller malting facilities and hops farms are popping up across the country in locations where the weather cooperates. In Massachusetts, there are a few small hop farms, mostly run by individual breweries and not yielding enough to support year-round brewing. There is also at least one malting facility.

Valley Malt is run by a husband and wife team in Hadley who recognized an obstacle for brewers who wanted to make a truly local beer with locally grown ingredients. They began malting both two-row and six-row barley and by 2010 had partnered with local farmers to plant twenty-six acres. During harvest season, they are able to turn out one ton of malt per week.

There is a lot to look forward to in the years to come with the return to brewing with local ingredients.

Beer Travel

Traveling from brewery to brewery is more than just drinking. It's a whole experience of discovering a new town, state, or country. For us, it's a privilege when people share their stories and we're able to make new friends with like-minded people at the bar.

Traveling to a brewery rather than your local store for a six-pack can open up new worlds. Breweries offer a chance to try a beer only available on draft or brews that do not have a distribution network. There may be new foods to try and new local stories to hear. You can see firsthand the work that went into a brewery and meet the people who work there.

As the American craft beer movement grows, so does the desire of drinkers to learn even more and to pry into the process behind their favorite beers. Breweries, it seems, are happy to oblige, offering experiences that go well beyond popping the top on a bottle.

Brewery tours are not new, of course. Back in the late 1800s, Anheuser-Busch recognized that consumers were interested in a behind-the-scenes look at the process and created a tour attraction at their flagship brewery in St. Louis, which is still popular. According to brewery officials, roughly 350,000 people toured the 142-acre complex in 2009, learning the history of Budweiser and its sister beers, seeing decades' worth of advertising and company trivia, and ending with a fresh sample.

The traditional tour follows this model: a view of the brewing system, a quick history of the place, a sample or two of whatever is on tap, and the chance to buy a T-shirt at the gift counter. But today, some folks have put a new spin on brewery touring.

Jim Koch, president of the Boston Beer Company, which produces the Samuel Adams line of beers, has for years been making an annual trip to Germany to select and harvest hops. You may have spotted one of those excursions in a Samuel Adams commercial. A few years ago folks at the company figured out that others would be interested in joining him on his trips, visiting the fields and centuries-old breweries and learning about beer in the place that perfected it. So a few years back, Boston Beer partnered with Abercrombie and Kent, a travel company, to create a weeklong excursion to Bavaria's beer country. The itinerary included visits to various biergartens, the centuries-old Stanglmair Farm and Hops Field just north of Munich, and the Weihenstephan Brewery, which dates back to the year 1040.

Koch told us that there were no immediate plans to do another such trip, which cost about $3,000 per person, but that his company would focus its efforts closer to home through a partnership with a luxury hotel in Boston. In addition to a stay at the hotel, participants get a private tour of the company's Jamaica Plain neighborhood brewery, where one of the brewers, not the usual tour guide, will show off the facilities and lead a tasting in the barrel room, a space usually closed to the public. Samuel Adams merchandise and a beer dinner with a brewery expert are included.

"Just like baby boomers adopted wine, their kids are adopting beer, and the parallels are extraordinary and enormous," Koch explained. "People want a better experience with their beer."

But the microbreweries still offer the most intimate experiences. The Woodstock Inn, a New Hampshire brewpub, began offering weekend packages within a year after opening its brewery in 1995, both to capitalize on the growing popularity of craft beer and to drum up business during the off-season, said owner Scott Rice. Their brewer weekends offer guests a chance to get inside the brewhouse and work on a commercial system. It's great fun and a chance for homebrewers to try their hand at something a little bigger. Guests can take part in every step of the brewing process, including the messy work of removing hundreds of pounds of processed grain from the mash tun, where grain and water are mixed.

Other breweries across the country offer similar packages with varying specifics. For example, Dogfish Head Craft Brewed Ales, a Delaware-based brewery, has partnered with a local inn where visitors are welcomed with amenities like beer soap and a library of brewing books. A tour of the brewery is also included.

In the Pacific Northwest, Rogue Ales, one of the more celebrated American craft breweries, has a six-bedroom house on its forty-two-acre hops farm in Independence, Oregon. Brett Joyce, president of the brewery, said that staying there gives visitors a chance to better

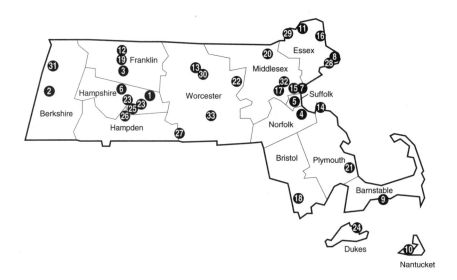

BREWERY LOCATIONS

book page

BREWERY LOCATIONS
book page

experience one of beer's main ingredients. The farm even hosts weddings. Farther south in the San Diego area, Stone Brewing Co. just bought a hotel that it plans to refurbish and offer as part of its brewery experience. The bottom line is that beer, the people who brew it, and those that love it can no longer be considered second-class citizens of the drinks world.

This is the new golden age of beer, and traveling to these breweries gives us a better understanding of where the American beer scene has come from and where it is going.

How to Use This Book

While not as celebrated as states like Colorado or Oregon, Massachusetts is a brewing powerhouse. This book is intended to serve as a guide to the working breweries and brewpubs of the state that offer tours to the general public.

It would be difficult to include the entire history, beer offerings, and personnel of each brewery in every entry, but we've strived to provide a snapshot of each place, a bit of flavor, and enough information to interest in you in visiting in person. If you have a question when you arrive at any particular brewery, just ask whoever is behind the bar or the brewers themselves. Folks who work in the brewing industry are mostly a friendly lot. They are usually eager to talk about their business in the hope that the word about good craft beer will spread far and wide.

As has been the practice in other books in this series, we're not going to hit you over the head with beer jargon or uber-technical terms. This is a travel guide, not a homebrewer's recipe book. We will address certain things along the way and have included a beer glossary in the back of the book (courtesy of our friend and fellow author Lew Bryson), but if you are looking for specifics on IBUs or a beer's Plato, or even yeast strains or hops varieties, it is best to save your questions for when you visit the brewery in person.

This book is split into eight parts. We've divided the state by regions—Western, Central, Merrimack Valley, Greater Boston Area, Coastal, and Cape Cod and the Islands. We've also included chapters on contract brewers who use in-state locations, breweries in neighboring Rhode Island (with too few to garner its own book), and a chapter on the larger craft breweries, Boston Beer Company (makers of Samuel Adams) and the Harpoon Brewery.

Each chapter begins with a little history of the region, what makes it unique from other parts of the state, and is peppered with attractions we suggest checking out while in the area. These range from the historic to the downright weird. We've included a list of bars and restaurants that serve a good variety of craft brews. When possible we visited those places in person for a pint or two, but in other cases had to rely on the recommendations of locals who we know and trust. These are listed after each brewery profile. There are many that we did not include, and if you're looking for a place, the best thing to do is ask while you're at the brewery. After all, those folks want a night off now and again and they will know where to get a good pint.

There are also lodging recommendations. In most cases, to stick with the theme of locally owned businesses and places with character, we largely ignored the chain hotels. However, there are a few that we've included, either because there were no alternatives within close distance to breweries or they were just plain cool.

During your research and travels in Massachusetts, it is possible that you will come across other breweries or brewpubs that are not included in this book. We're certainly aware of their existence, and even visited a few of them, but did not write full profiles because they either do not offer tours to the public, they were not yet open for business as of this book's deadline, or because they don't meet the true standards of brewing.

One of these is Mystic Brewing of Chelsea. Founder and brewer Bryan Greenhagen calls his operation a "Fermentorium," because the first few steps of the brewing process are done at remote locations and the wort is shipped to Mystic for fermentation. "It's been working out well so far," Greenhagen told us. "The best part is that our saison is being mashed and boiled at a genuine farmhouse brewery, while fermentation, blending, and bottling is done in the urban environment." We wish Greenhagen all the best, have enjoyed his beers, and should he open a full brewery down the line (a plan being discussed), we'll include it in future editions.

There are other examples of brewery names as restaurants. Logan Airport is a beer-based transportation hub of its own with Harpoon, Beer Works, and Cisco all represented (although the names are leased out to third parties and no brewing is done on premises). Out west, John Harvard's Brewery & Ale House operates a satellite location at Jiminy Peak in Hancock, but again no beer is made on premises.

Since we began research on this book, several other people have expressed interest or even filed papers with the intent of opening a brewery or brewpub, meaning that soon there will be a larger wealth of local beer options for visitors and residents alike. We'll be keeping tabs on them on the website www.beerbriefing.com and will update as new breweries and brewpubs open. As this book went to press, there were several developments within the Massachusetts craft beer scene.

- Ben Howe, currently of Cambridge Brewing Company, is launching Enlightenment Brewery in Lowell. Those who have tried the brewery's inaugural batches are impressed, and Howe's brews should be worth seeking out once they hit shelves.

- High and Mighty Beer Company, which has been contracting out of Paper City, is moving towards opening a facility of its own in Easthampton.

- Matthew Steinberg of Blatant Brewery will be taking over at the former Amherst Brewing Company location, giving this popular gypsy brewery a place to call home.

It's also good to call in advance of a visit. Brewers take vacations just like the rest of us, and while there might be a sign on the door alerting the locals to the fact, we don't want you driving a long distance only to find they'll reopen next Monday. As for tours, you'll see that many offer them by appointment or only on certain days.

It should go without saying, but please do not drink and drive. Know your limitations, and if you decide that you're having too much fun and want to stay for a few more (and hey, who hasn't been there?) just have the bartender call you a cab. We took turns driving while working on this trip, and it helped not only with the writing, but gave us peace of mind knowing that we would be getting home safe each and every night.

Now it's time for you to begin your Massachusetts beer odyssey. Go thirsty, with an open mind, and enjoy every pint. Cheers!

Biggest of the Craft

There are more than two thousand breweries in the country today, the high-est numbers the nation has seen since the advent of Prohibition. Massachusetts is home to two of the largest craft breweries. Both are in Boston.

Boston Beer Company, makers of the Samuel Adams line of beers, has both its corporate headquarters in the city as well as a smaller brewery tourist destination, with a gift shop, in the Jamaica Plain neighborhood. Boston Beer is the largest American-owned brewery. However, most of the beer the brewery produces—more than two million barrels—comes from facilities in Ohio and Pennsylvania.

The other craft brew giant is Harpoon, the brewery that has state license number 1, awarded by the commonwealth after Massachusetts's brewing scene was dormant for longer than most can remember. Harpoon does much of its brewing on the waterfront (they also have a brewery in Vermont) and is currently among the nation's ten largest craft breweries.

Numbers aside, both breweries are sources of pride for the city. They are must-see destinations for tourists and highly admired by the greater brewing community.

Boston Beer Company/Samuel Adams

SAMUEL ADAMS

30 Germania Street, Boston MA 02130
617-368-5080 • www.samueladams.com

Of all the American brewers currently working, Jim Koch is perhaps the most recognizable. Like Pavlov's dog, TV viewers have come to expect him on the screen as soon as they hear first electric-guitar licks of George Thorogood and the Destroyers belting out "Who Do You Love."

Those commercials showing Koch strolling hops farms in Germany, employees smiling and drinking a beer on Friday afternoon, or brewers talking about the creation of a new beer have helped consumers connect with Samuel Adams, the flagship line of beers produced by the Boston Beer Company. And it has been accomplished without the very gimmicks that Koch rails against when talking about the big brewers. No slapstick humor, no bikini-clad girls, no talking animals. Just beer and the people who make it.

Koch (pronounced cook), the famed founder of the Boston Beer Company, is credited with shepherding the brewery from a small operation that started in his kitchen, when he went from bar to bar with bottles in his briefcase, to the largest American craft brewery, now making more than two million barrels of beer a year.

Beers Brewed: Boston Lager, Light, Boston Ale, Pale Ale, Cherry Wheat, Cream Stout, Scotch Ale, Black Lager, Brown Ale, Honey Porter, Irish Red Ale, Blackberry Witbier, Coastal Wheat, Dunkelweizen, Harvest Pumpkin Ale, Bonfire Rauchbier, White Ale, Rustic Saison, East-West Kolsch, Latitude 48 IPA, Cranberry Lambic, Black & Brew Coffee Stout, Noble Pils, Summer Ale, Octoberfest, Winter Lager, Infinium, Utopias, Double Bock, Imperial White, Imperial Stout, Wee Heavy, New World, American Kriek, Stony Brook Red, Thirteenth Hour, Chocolate Bock, Old Fezziwig Ale, Holiday Porter.

This number is considered small in the brewing world, especially when you consider that the large breweries produce tens of millions of barrels each year under different names that share the same corporate ownership. This includes brands like Blue Moon, which contributes to the corporate bottom line of Coors and is not considered craft, although it is marketed that way.

Koch said he still enjoys coming to work each and every day and shows the same passion and spirit with new brewery projects as he did two and a half decades ago, when he started peddling Boston Lager throughout Beantown.

On days when he is at the company's small research and development brewery in Boston and tourists catch a glimpse of him, you'd think Mick

Jagger had just shown up. People line up to shake his hand, pose for pictures, pepper him with brewing questions, and ask for autographs.

Up close and away from the crowds, however, he comes across as a regular, aw-shucks kind of guy, with a mid-tempo gravelly voice and pleasant smile. He's a natural salesman and has gotten his brewery facts down to simple points that clearly illustrate not only the importance but also the size of his brewery.

"The big guys spill more per year than we make," is one familiar Koch line.

He's proud to talk about his brewing heritage. In case you hadn't heard, he's a fifth-generation brewer. Boston Lager is based on a recipe that was in the family line and given to him by his father. He brewed it for the first time, like so many homebrewers before and after him, in his kitchen.

While it took hard work and determination to launch back in the mid-1980s, Koch had a strategic advantage over others who launched around the same time that propelled him to the top of the craft sooner than anyone could have expected: The man is incredibly smart. He holds BA, MBA, and JD degrees from Harvard University and has brought his keen business sense to the brewing world and watched as it blossomed into a company now traded on the New York Stock Exchange.

When he first started in 1984, Koch was armed—brewingwise—with little more than that recipe. Like many homebrewers, he could make batches for sampling, but to get his product to market he needed equipment. So, he took a different route from other fledgling breweries at the time and contracted out space at a Pennsylvania brewery. Using that equipment allowed him to spend more time marketing and selling the beer. Clearly that strategy worked out and today a brewery contracting from existing space is commonplace.

That's not to say the early Boston Beer Company did not have a home. Koch and crew leased space in the long-closed Haffenreffer Brewery from a community group in what was then the rough-and-tumble Jamaica Plain neighborhood. It's a grand redbrick complex that transports modern visitors back to the glory days of brewing, when the craftsmanship of the building was just as important as the beer. The thick walls, towering smokestack, and touch of German sensibilities still stand today. Koch brewed his first batch in that building in

The Pick: Thirteenth Hour is a stout in the brewery's Barrel Room Collection. Handsomely bottled in a cage-and-cork finished vessel that looks like an elongated brew kettle, this Belgian-inspired brew pours jet black. As the aromas one would expect, chocolate and coffee, begin to reveal themselves, there is a slight tang that emerges from the brettanomyces and lacticobacillus yeasts that have permeated the oak barrels where the beer ferments. The result is a marriage of flavors from spicy to sweet, bitter to savory. A beer to be savored and sipped as time slips away.

1988 and since then the two-tiered, copper-clad system continually produces batches and serves many purposes, including research and development. It also turns out the much sought after, 27-percent ABV, barrel-aged Utopias. When the beer is still in barrels, waiting to be bottled in ceramic vessels shaped like brew kettles, visitors who catch a glimpse will act like they've seen a treasured work of art. The brewery also brews batches of Boston Lager to be delivered to Doyle's, a famed local saloon that was the brewery's first account.

During the early days of occupying the brewery, Koch said break-ins were routine and vandalism was a problem. Eventually a solution was worked up. Each night a case of beer was placed in an unlocked truck. The next morning, the beer would be gone, and the building was untouched. This continued for a while.

"One morning we came, and the beer was still there. We actually got worried for a minute wondering if these guys were okay," Koch said with a laugh.

Today the neighborhood has been gentrified and families walk the tight streets, occasionally pointing the way for comfortably dressed tourists heading towards the brewery from the subway. The rest of the complex has filled out as well, with several businesses occupying the old Haffenreffer space.

When it comes to Koch, there are some who gripe about his shrewd business dealings, and documentaries like the agenda-pushing *Beer Wars* made him out to be a ruthless owner who would not help a former partner out. But the overall fact remains that most of his fellow brewers and owners hold him in high regard.

During the hops shortage a few years back, Boston Beer sold brewers around the country hops cones at cost. Others are still talking about the generosity Koch and his brewery showed two years ago at the Craft Brewers Conference, where visitors were greeted with a belly-busting New England clambake and bottomless kegs.

Koch knows what it means to start a small business. He traversed the pitfalls and unexpected turns and threats from outside and within, so in 2008, he started a program that would provide microloans to Boston-area businesses, helping them get a leg up and on the road to success. Partnering with ACCION USA, the nation's largest nonprofit microloan provider to small business owners, the brewery has helped a handful of businesses over the years. The program also holds a number of "speed coaching" events, seminars designed to provide advice, feedback, and a sounding board for new ideas.

Koch has expanded the program into other cities, such as New York, and has even begun reaching out to smaller brewers and encouraging them to apply for loans. A winning brewery also receives the "Samuel Adams Brewing and Business Experienceship." This, according to Koch, is tailored to the brewery's business needs and includes additional coaching, an invitation to the Boston Beer Company Negotiation and Selling Skills classes, financial support to set up at the Great American Beer Festival, and at least one trip to Boston. Koch was clear, however, that the breweries that receive the loans and ones that win the "Experienceship" would remain autonomous and not be a part of his brewery or business.

"We just want to help," he said. "I am happy with what I have."

Those are just a few examples of how large and profitable the brewery has become. It got there through some smart investing, a strong marketing push, and of course, being a flavorful beer. Samuel Adams Boston Lager has propelled the Boston Beer Company to become one of the largest breweries in the country.

The success of Boston Lager in particular has helped the American craft beer scene overall. It has been a gateway beer, if you will, enticing people who traditionally went for large-scale-produced beers that rely on "beechwood aging" or "triple-hops brewing" to try something new.

Liking what they tasted, consumers began broadening their beer horizons, trying beers made in their area or other craft beer on store shelves and branching out to other Samuel Adams beers, including the perennial favorite Summer Ale, beer-geek inspiring Utopias, and wickedly delicious Imperial White.

The brewery was ahead of the curve in releasing its own signature glass several years ago and even partnered with a New York City–based butcher to create a "new" cut of beef to be paired with Boston Lager. The company's small brewery in Boston (most of the production is done in Ohio and Pennsylvania) is one of the city's top tourist attractions. Simply put, it is one of the most recognizable beer brands in the country.

For as large as Boston Beer has become, Koch is determined to keep inventing, keep pushing boundaries, and keep trying to remember where he came from.

In the last few years the brewery has released its Barrel Room Collection, four beers derived from a 7-percent alcohol beer Koch calls "Kosmic Mother Funk, or KMF." The barrel-aged beers—American Kriek; New World Tripel; Thirteenth Hour, a Belgian-style stout; and Stony Brook Red—have received high praise from beer aficionados lucky enough to taste them. (Currently they are only available in limited quantities, although the brewery is well stocked.)

Given their size and the passion and talent of the many brewers on staff, Boston Beer turns out a dizzying number of beers, both established and new. Every season has a variety pack that is filled with tasty brews. There are limited-edition holiday beers, some which are only available at sporting events, and still others that show up on shelves and then disappear forever. Press material supplied by the brewery runs seven pages long with a list of their beers.

Perhaps the biggest thing to come out of the brewery in years and a source of great anticipation is the collaboration beer Samuel Adams brewed with Weihenstephan, the world's oldest brewery. Called Infinium, it is brewed in the Reinheitsgebot tradition, or German Purity Law, which states that beer is to be made with just four ingredients: water, malt, hops, and yeast. Koch poured samples during a recent event at the brewery and the unique beer revealed itself to be champagne-like, with a sweet taste that had a slight spice finish. "This is a true collaboration. It's our input, it's their input," said Koch. "No one has ever done this. It was a lot of fun. It was crazy."

While others who played key roles in launching and promoting this modern American craft beer movement have begun to retire, such as Fritz Maytag of Anchor Brewing, or are talking about handing the reins to the next generation, like Ken Grossman of Sierra Nevada Brewing Company, Koch said recently that he has no plans to step aside or slow down anytime soon.

"I love doing what I am doing," he said. "I don't want to work for anyone else."

As for passing along the keys to the kingdom, Koch has several children, including two adults—one who works as a high school guidance counselor and the other who is a public defender. In fact, a beer first brewed for his daughter's wedding later became the brewery's spring offering, Noble Pils. But, at this point, there are no plans for them to rejoin the family business. "I've always encouraged them to find their own path and they did," he said. "They both worked here and they know how to brew. But, they found their own careers."

So the company will remain in his hands for the foreseeable future. Koch holds all of the Company's Class B Common Stock, meaning that although there is a board of directors and shareholders to answer to, any decision regarding the brewery must receive his blessing first.

He tries to stay true to the home-brewing roots that got him to where he is today and the customers who kept the brewery afloat in the early years. The Samuel Adams Long Shot Competition encourages homebrewers to submit recipes that are judged by industry professionals. Winners are brewed, bottled, and released in Samuel Adams variety packs.

Amid all the conversation about barrel numbers, Koch seems amused, bewildered, but proud at how large his company has become.

"It's both surreal and sobering," he said. "When we first started, I wanted to get to five thousand barrels and eight employees. Obviously we blew that away." Today the company employs nearly eight hundred people.

One thing has not changed. "It is still the same beer, made in the same way, with the same ingredients," he said.

Boston Beer Company/Samuel Adams

Opened: 1984.

Owner: Jim Koch.

Brewers: Jim Koch, David Grinnell, David Sipes, Bob Cannon, Dean Gianocostas, Jennifer Glanville, Bert Boyce, Grant Wood, and Andrew Lamont.

System: Pub brewing system, 10-barrel, steam jacketed, and manual valves.

Production: 2,259,000 barrels at all breweries in 2010.

Tours: Monday through Thursday, 10 A.M. to 3 P.M.; Friday, 10 A.M. to 5:30 P.M.; Saturday, 10 A.M. to 3 P.M. Tours depart approximately every 45 minutes and last about 1 hour. A donation of $2 benefits local charities. Groups of more than twenty call (617) 368-5256 to schedule a private tour, available Monday through Thursday, 3:30 or 4 P.M.

Take-out beer: Samuel Adams Barrel Room Collection and specialty styles.

Extras: Gift shop. Open house offered once a month. To learn more, sign up for the online newsletter: www.samueladams.com/Promotions/Contact/contact_ newsletter.aspx.

Special considerations: Handicapped-accessible.

Parking: There is a small parking lot, but it's usually full. We recommend using public transportation; the brewery is within walking distance from the Stony Brook stop on the MBTA Orange Line.

Harpoon Brewery

306 Northern Avenue, Boston, MA 02210
617-547-9551 • www.harpoonbrewery.com

What is currently one of the largest craft breweries in America started off as a school report back in the 1980s. Harpoon Brewery's cofounder, Rich Doyle, was in his second year at Harvard Business School when he prepared a report on microbreweries and what it would take to open one in Boston. Doyle repurposed the report into a business plan, partnered with his old friend Dan Kenary, and set out to open what would be the first microbrewery in Massachusetts.

"We have brewing license number 1 from 1986," said Kenary, noting that Harpoon was the first brewery to open in the state after a long, dry period. They opened shop in an area that was once a naval base on Boston's waterfront and have steadily expanded since that first batch.

"The first five to eight years were really hard," said Doyle. "I don't want to candy-coat it. I look back on twenty-five years and some stuff was not that much fun, but I am proud we are still in business. It is a testament to how hard we fought and how creative we all were and how determined we were to succeed."

In the beginning they focused on ales, and the beer that first grabbed customers' attention was a mild English ale. In 1992, they introduced an impressive India Pale Ale as a summer seasonal. The next year it became a year-round release and now Harpoon IPA is the brewery's flagship beer.

Harpoon began with 5,200 square feet of space and now occupies 47,000 square feet. When one factors in outdoor areas, the brewery is closer to 100,000 square feet. It is an impressive industrial building constructed for naval operations and is indeed tall and long enough to fit ships. Visitors traverse ribbed metal steps between fermentation tanks and brew kettles to climb down three stories from the tasting room to the concrete floor.

Currently, Kenary said they are adding an additional 50,000 barrels to their existing 125,000-barrel capacity and tripling their racking capacity. Harpoon purchased a second brewery in Vermont

Beers Brewed: Harpoon IPA, Harpoon Dark, Harpoon Cider, Leviathan Imperial IPA, UFO Hefeweizen, UFO White, UFO Raspberry Hefeweizen, Celtic Ale, Summer Beer, Bohemian Pilsner, Octoberfest, UFO Pumpkin, UFO Pale Ale, Grateful Harvest Cranberry Ale, Winter Warmer, Chocolate Stout, Leviathan Barleywine, Leviathan Quad, Leviathan Uber-bock, Leviathan Imperial Rye, Leviathan Triticus.

that also features tours and tastings and produces about 60,000 barrels of beer per year.

The current tasting and tourism room in Boston, a hike up a steep flight of stairs, is a wood-planked floor affair that is reminiscent of a historic yet comfortable neighborhood bar.

Bottles, cans, and other brewing memorabilia donated by staff and visitors take up shelf space, and large picture windows look out to the top level of the brewhouse. More than five thousand people visit each month.

The Pick: The Imperial Rye is part of the brewery's Leviathan Series. The addition of rye to this English-style ale brings an added depth, a thicker mouthfeel, and the overwhelming feeling of satisfaction with each swallow.

The brewery is relatively close to downtown, something Kenary and Doyle said was important to their business plan. They cited breweries in Europe that were not located directly in villages, but on the outskirts, accessible for everyone and serving as hubs. That's why they waited nearly six months for the waterfront space to become available.

A quarter century later, the wait paid off, as the brewery is in easy walking distance (with comfortable shoes) from the South Station and remains one of Boston's more popular tourist destinations. Harpoon is so comfortable, in fact, that they recently signed a fifty-year lease with the city that will keep them in their current marine industrial park location. With their location on city-owned land, officials tout Harpoon as a hometown success story, something the mayor does on regular occasions. "People love manufacturing businesses and we can keep jobs in town," said Kenary. "That's important."

He also pointed out that for a city like Boston, with its bustling tourism and convention industry, having a brewery that is within walking distance of hotels is a selling point. "To be honest, they love us here," said Kenary.

Upon arrival visitors can chose pours from various taps, ranging from experimental beers and familiar standbys to the offerings of the big-beer Leviathan Series. With the number of visitors each month, there are plans, Kenary said, to move the tasting room from the east side of the building to the west side. The brewery is also going to install a 10-barrel pilot system to test new beers that could eventually become part of the official lineup.

One well-known Harpoon beer, in fact, started out as an experiment. Doyle said that a few years ago the brewery produced a raspberry lambic and at a summer festival noticed that patrons were mixing it with Harpoon's hefeweizen. Soon, UFO (Unfiltered Offering) Raspberry Hefeweizen joined the lineup as a popular summer seasonal.

Spend even a short amount of time at the brewery and it becomes clear that the employees who work here love what they do. Part of that is because it's an environment that encourages creativity. Brewers and nonbrewers alike are welcome to pitch ideas, and many are tested with a few even getting to market. "If we like it, we get behind it and push it," said Kenary.

Another great thing about working at Harpoon is the trips. After five, eight, and twelve years of service, employees are taken on a company European vacation, with tours to breweries and a chance to reconnect with coworkers outside of a work environment.

One important thing to note about Harpoon is that it is the largest brewery in Massachusetts. Some might think of a certain patriot-named brewery as being larger, but Boston Beer Company, makers of the Samuel Adams brand, brews most of its beers in large breweries in Pennsylvania and Ohio.

The Harpoon Brewery has stayed true to its roots and several years ago launched Harpoon Helps, a philanthropic arm of the company that donates thousands of dollars in merchandise and many barrels of beer to New England charities as well as volunteer hours. For a brewery that began life in a classroom, Harpoon has grown into an impressive operation that is an undeniable asset to the American craft beer scene. Customers, in turn, have responded with loyalty and passion. To see the cavalcade of visitors to the breweries and endless pints poured at bars up and down the East Coast, in the words of Doyle, "is why we got into this and are still in business."

"We make great beer and welcome beer lovers," he said. "That's what we're about."

Harpoon Brewery

Opened: 1986.

Owners: Rich Doyle and Dan Kenary.

Brewers: Al Marzi (Chief of Brewing Operations) and Todd Charbonneau and Scott Shirley (Senior Brewers).

System: 120-barrel Huppmann Brewhouse.

Production: 170,000–175,000 barrels in 2011.

Tours: Monday through Friday, 2 P.M. and 4 P.M.; Saturday, 10:30 A.M. to 5 P.M., every half hour; Sunday, 11 AM to 3 P.M., every half hour.

Take-out beer: Bottles and growlers.

Extras: Brewery store. 5:30 Club. Seasonal festivals.

Special considerations: Handicapped-accessible.

Parking: Limited visitor spots available. Public parking on street and in garage across the street.

Other area beer sites: See page 106.

The Massachusetts Brewers Guild
by President Rob Martin

Massachusetts is home to some of the world's best craft beer, and in 2007, brewers from the state came together to form the Massa-  chusetts Brewers Guild. The guild is a 501(c)(6) nonprofit corporation, organized for the purposes of promoting craft brewing and protecting the interests of craft brewers in the commonwealth. Membership is open to all Massachusetts breweries licensed by the federal Tax and Trade Bureau and the commonwealth's Alcoholic Beverage Control Commission. Currently there are more than fifty brewing licenses issued, which include brewpubs, farm breweries, and manufacturers.

In just a few short years, the Massachusetts Brewers Guild has become an extremely effective voice for promoting the interests of all the brewers in Massachusetts for a wide variety of topics. Our mission is to "promote craft brewing and protect the interests of craft brewers in Massachusetts." This takes shape through our legislative efforts, our promotion of local beer though our guild-run festivals, and our ability to create a social network of brewers in Massachusetts where each individual brewery feels part of the whole. This unity ultimately has produced a powerful voice across the spectrum of our activities

When it comes to legislative diligence, our guild has become so effective that we have become the model for guilds around the nation. We have worked tirelessly to improve the business climate for brewers in Massachusetts and whether it is improving licensing procedures, defining who and what craft brewers are, franchise-law reform, or general legislative outreach, our singular voice as a guild has opened many more doors than could have been opened individually.

Regarding promotion, we have offered opportunities to all Massachusetts brewers to participate in a variety of events that focus solely on their products. Whether it is a Massachusetts-only beer table at the

Massachusetts Package Store Association's trade show, the Massachusetts Brewers Guild Beer Festival featuring only Massachusetts brews, or the Ultimate Beer Dinner featuring local beer paired with local food, the guild has created an atmosphere where a rising tide lifts all boats.

Socially, we have two open meetings a year where all the Massachusetts brewery owners and employees are encouraged to come socialize, share ideas, and continue to create and strengthen the bond that has made us so successful in our first four years.

We as a guild look forward to many more years of continued growth in the craft beer category and we understand that our collective effort and our strength as a guild will be one of the determining factors in our ultimate success.

Western Massachusetts

Country roads winding through gently rolling farmlands, river valleys, and quintessential New England villages, and then climbing dizzily up into the mountains: These are scenes you will encounter as you drive through Western Massachusetts. While the rest of the state seems to face directly eastward to the sea at all times, the western half of Massachusetts maintains a more rugged, remote feel. But as rustic as it might appear, it's also a reputable artistic and cultural community. For the purposes of this book, Western Massachusetts is made up of two distinct areas: the Pioneer Valley and the Berkshires.

The Pioneer Valley is the land surrounding the Connecticut River, which cuts its way through the heart of the state. It's a fertile, flat area—made up of farmlands that feel almost Midwestern—that supplies the state with the majority of its produce and livestock. This is also the home of Springfield, the third-largest city in the state, which straddles the river and was originally a mill town, with a history of heavy manufacturing.

The valley was originally settled in the 1600s by farmers looking to utilize the land, but by the early 1800s, industrialists made their way there when they recognized the power of the river and developed textile and paper mills along its banks.

These newly wealthy industrialists then founded what is now the pride of the region—its many world-class colleges and universities. The famous five heavy hitters are Smith College, Mount Holyoke College, Amherst College, Hampshire College, and the enormous University of Massachusetts–Amherst. This profusion of intellectual activity brings youth and vitality to the region, with thousands of students arriving every fall.

In the heart of all of this is Northampton (known as "Noho"), the home of Smith College. This cultural powerhouse has an atmospheric Main Street lined with bars, cafes, and bookshops, and it holds many yearly events such as art exhibitions and independent film festivals. Another popular spot is nearby Amherst, a classic, quaint small town infused with the energy of a big college.

- **Deerfield** (www.historic-deerfield.org) is a good place to get a sense of the area's past. It is a small town originally settled more than three hundred years ago and still chock-full of houses built in the eighteenth and nineteenth centuries. The town itself has been designated a National Historic Landmark Village, and thirteen of its historic houses, built from 1730 to 1850, can be visited on tours run by a local organization called Historic Deerfield for a sense of what it was like to live in an early New England settlement.

Deerfield is also considered the gateway to the Berkshires, where options for biking, canoeing, camping, and cross-country skiing start to grow in ample abundance.

- **Look Park** (www.lookpark.org), in nearby Florence, has 157 acres of Victorian-style parklands and is a great place that includes trails, miniature golf, a small zoo, and paddleboats. If you're feeling adventurous, the Deerfield River is popular for its white-water rafting and kayaking and is a healthy way to work up an appetite before a big brewpub dinner.

Heading north from Deerfield, you begin to enter the Berkshires. Popular as a summer getaway for city-dwellers, the Berkshires also have a more bohemian, artistic side, with many world-class music and theater options, art museums and galleries, and enough nature activities to keep any outdoor enthusiast happy for weeks.

The Berkshires themselves are roughly divided into two regions, north and south. The Southern Berkshires have the reputation of being a summer playground for the urban wealthy looking for an escape from Boston and New York. Manicured lawns surrounding sprawling mansions (known as "Berkshire Cottages") abound in well-heeled towns like Lenox, and a sophisticated artistic culture prevails alongside the rustic sense of being in the country. While here, be sure to visit Tanglewood, summer home of the Boston Symphony Orchestra, (www.bso .org) for a musical afternoon picnic, or spend an evening at Shakespeare & Company (www.shakespeare.org), a world-class regional theater known for having famous movie and television actors drop in for a week or two of performances. Restaurants here are abundant, as well as opportunities for boutique shopping or visits to local art galleries.

While traveling through, be sure to stop in Stockbridge if you can bear the tourists. This is where Norman Rockwell spent the last twenty-five years of his life, getting inspiration from the country landscape and old-fashioned Main Street downtown.

- **Norman Rockwell Museum** (www.nrm.org) is a slice of old-time Americana, where you can see the world's largest collection of Rockwell paintings, including his famous illustrations for *The Saturday Evening Post*. You can also view his well-preserved home and attached barn, where he did most of his painting.

As you travel in this part of the state you can follow the Mohawk Trail (www.mohawktrail.com), a former Native American footpath turned into a scenic byway for autos in 1914. Now State Route 2, it's speckled with motor lodges and Native American trading posts. The 63 miles of country road hits its scenic peak during the brilliant fall foliage season, although the panoramic views are worthwhile any time of year.

As you head north, the countryside becomes more rugged as you climb in elevation towards craggier mountains.

- **Mount Greylock State Reservation** (www.mass.gov/dcr/parks/mtGreylock) appeals to outdoorsy types with opportunities for hiking, biking, and camping. Or if you'd rather explore from the comfort of your car, drive to the peak of Mount Greylock, the highest point in the state, with an elevation of 3,491 feet. You can take in the view that reaches into five states on a clear day, or visit the Mount Greylock War Memorial, a 92-foot-high memorial tower dedicated to veterans.

Although more remote, the Northern Berkshires still has culture in spades.

- **Massachusetts Museum of Contemporary Art** (www.massmoca .org), in North Adams, is a formerly depressed mill town turned arts destination. North Adams has dozens of galleries springing up in the wake of the success of the museum, which is one of the finest in the country. Or head to nearby Williamstown, ringed by dramatic mountains, for more art museums and theater festivals.

As a whole, Western Massachusetts blends the personalities of urban summer visitors, with their infusions of money and highbrow culture, and the youth and energy of the college crowd. The whole region is a mix of beautiful scenery, friendly villages, and an artistic culture that is truly unique.

There are plenty of affordable options for lodging in the Springfield area, including budget motels, as well as bed-and-breakfasts in smaller price ranges. You can pick from any of the major chains to find the best place to suit your budget.

- **Sheraton Springfield Monarch Place Hotel** (www.sheraton.com) is the largest hotel in the city, located in the heart of downtown with 325 guest rooms to choose from.

- **Naomi's Inn Bed and Breakfast** (www.naomisinn.net), a small but nicely appointed restored Victorian home, is the perfect choice if you're looking for something a little more intimate.

- **Allen House Inn** (www.allenhouse.com) is a bed-and-breakfast in Amherst, within walking distance of downtown.

- **The Black Walnut Inn** (www.blackwalnutinn.com) is a Federal-style brick bed-and-breakfast on an acre of property in Amherst.

- **The Hotel Northampton** (www.hotelnorthampton.com) is a charming Colonial Revival grand hotel in Northampton.

While in the Berkshires, you can stay anywhere from a budget campsite to a world-famous luxury resort.

- **Canyon Ranch in the Berkshires** (www.canyonranch.com) is a health and wellness resort in Lenox. Consider this only if money is no option.

- **The Red Lion Inn** (www.redlioninn.com), in Stockbridge, is the place to go if you want pure New England historic atmosphere. Built in 1773, it provides it in spades but is on the pricey side. Be sure to make reservations well in advance, because this is a highly popular tourist stopover point.

- **The Briarcliff Motel** (www.thebriarcliffmotel.com), a revamped 1960s-style motel in Great Barrington, is great if you're looking for something less expensive.

- **Apple Tree Inn** (www.appletree-inn.com), in Lenox, is an affordable option in a pricey area.

Here are some other interesting attractions worth visiting in Western Massachusetts.

- **Naismith Memorial Basketball Hall of Fame** (www.hoophall.com) in Springfield is a must-stop for all basketball fans. Springfield is where basketball was invented in 1891.

- **Dr. Seuss National Memorial Sculpture Garden** (www.catinthe hat.org) in Springfield is a good stop if you're traveling with kids, or just feeling a little whimsical. Theodore Seuss Geisel was born in Springfield in 1904 and incorporated many of the local sights into his famous books. Take some time to stroll through this park, where his most beloved creations are sculpted in bronze.

- **Emily Dickinson Homestead** (www.emilydickinsonmuseum.org) in Amherst is the house where the famous poet spent nearly her entire life. Her bedroom, where she composed many of her most famous poems, is the biggest draw.

- **Yankee Candle Flagship Store** (www.yankeecandle.com) in Deerfield is where the chain store began. You can wander through its warehouse-sized location for hours and take in the aromas.

- **Six Flags New England** (www.sixflags.com) in Agawam boasts more than one hundred rides and thrills. But be forewarned: The park closes for the cold New England winters, leaving it open from April through October only, with weekend-only hours in the shoulder months.

- **Sterling and Francine Clark Art Institute** (www.clarkart.edu) in nearby Williamstown is one of the highest-rated small museums in the country.

- **Williamstown Theatre Festival** (www.wtfestival.org) is the place to take in a show, and you might be surprised to see your favorite film or television actor on the stage.

- **Hancock Shaker Village** (www.hancockshakervillage.org) near Pittsfield is a preserved nineteenth-century village that was one of the homes of the religious community famous for its furniture making and unusual religious beliefs.

Amherst Brewing Company

10 University Drive, Amherst, MA 01002
413-253-4400 • www.amherstbrewing.com

If you've visited the Amherst Brewing Company, known around here as ABC, double-check the address above before heading out for your next visit. That's because in mid-2011, the brewery moved from its former comfortable-but-cramped, multiroom and multi-level building off North Pleasant Street to its current location, a sprawling space that once housed a gym and a grocery store.

While the old location was just fine (they did go through three expansions, after all) one of the main reasons for the move was parking, according to brewer John Geraci. Given their location on a crowded thoroughfare with limited outside space, they were routinely busy, but also missing out on potential business. So when the new retail space became available a few blocks away, the owners decided to make the move. After cutting through the bureaucratic red tape, the move was a rather simple one.

The owners tried to replicate as much as they could from the old space to this new one, including brickwork on the exterior of the building and the paint and color scheme on the inside. Even the red neon Hampden Ale sign made the move and regained its place above the bar.

And how about that bar? Easily the highlight of the new brewery, the 100-foot copper-top bar with a leaflike pattern has front molding from African Sapele wood. It's impressive, it's comfortable, it's unique, and it's the perfect place to saddle up for some of Geraci's beers.

Since he came on board six years ago, he's tried to reinvent some recipes, improve others, and add his own to the mix. What you get is a solid lineup of ales and lagers that runs the rainbow of beer colors. Two beer engines mean a constant supply of fresh cask ale, and the brewery isn't afraid to put guest drafts on tap.

The new space also means expansion for the brewhouse, which was crammed into a small

Beers Brewed: Ace in the Hole Pilsner, Amity Street Dark Wheat, Cascade IPA, Honey Pilsner, Puffers Smoked Porter, Massatucky Brown, North Pleasant Pale Ale, Two Sisters Imperial Stout, and a variety of seasonal beers.

The Pick: The Honey Pilsner has everything a crisp pilsner should have: strong malts and a slight hop spice. But the addition of wildflower honey brings a sweetness that makes this beer delightful to drink, pint after pint.

ground-level space at the old location. They have already added two new 10-barrel fermentation tanks, with additional equipment expected in the coming months. "We've left room in the space and as time goes on we can increase overall barrelage," Geraci said.

The brewery's location in a college town brings both challenges and rewards. With a constant cycle of students and parents coming through, there are always new customers, but time must be taken to explain the beers, how they're made, and why dad can't get his familiar light lager. But there are also regulars who have made ABC their home bar, coming in week after week, forming bonds with the staff, giving feedback to Geraci, and running through the expansive pub menu.

That's another great thing about ABC: the food. If you leave hungry from this place it's your own fault. Large sandwiches and burgers piled high with fries and hearty dinner items like grilled tuna steak and pasta dishes ensure there is something for everyone.

It's a great place to catch a game on TV or visit for some local music. As was the tradition in the old place, the Amherst Jazz Orchestra has returned to play their regular gigs on the first and third Mondays of every month. Other musicians cycle through, including a strong number of funk bands.

"There is a lot of positive energy at this place," Geraci told us. "We're invigorated and people are happy to come here. They are really happy about the parking."

Amherst Brewing Company

Opened: 1997.

Owners: John Korpita, majority owner, and a group of investors.

Brewers: John Geraci and Shaun St. Clair.

System: 10-barrel system.

Production: 800 barrels in 2011.

Hours: Monday through Saturday, 11:30 A.M. to 1 A.M.; Sunday, 10 A.M. to 1 A.M. (including brunch).

Tours: By appointment.

Take-out beer: 64-ounce growlers.

Extras: Happy hour. Live music, with Amherst Jazz Orchestra on the first and third Monday of each month and occasionally other bands or DJs. Function room available for special events and parties. Pool room.

Special considerations: Handicapped-accessible.

Parking: 200+ space free lot.

Other area beer sites:

- **Hangar Pub & Grille** (55 University Drive, Amherst, 413-549-9464, www.wings overamherst.com) is across the street from the brewpub and has a good draft lineup, as well as a heart-stopping amount of wing choices.
- **Sierra Grille** (41 Strong Avenue #A, Northampton, 413-584-1150, www.sierra grille.net) has a great draft list and killer food.

Lefty's Brewing Company

301 Wells Street, Greenfield, MA 01301
413-475-3449 • www.leftysbrew.com

Before he was a brewer, Bill Goldfarb was a roofer. It so happened that there was another guy on the job with the same first name. After a while the boss was tired of shouting out "Bill" and having two people respond. So one day he pointed up to the two Bills working on the roof and dubbed the left-handed Goldfarb "Lefty." It stuck. When it came time to hang his own shingle, the name came along with him. He opened a nanobrewery in 2010, an operation typically defined as a brewery with equipment capable of producing no more than three barrels at a time.

Lefty's first brewery sat in a small storefront on a slow country road near the Massachusetts-Vermont border in the town of Bernardston. Inside that tiny two-barrel brewhouse, he set to work producing everything from English porter to pale ale. The community embraced Lefty and his tiny brewery, and sales were so strong during his first six months of operation that Goldfarb was already looking at larger equipment and a new space. The community is also big on food, so Lefty regularly hosted beer and food dinners on picnic tables in the parking lot. They were potluck affairs, and most dishes used Lefty's beers as at least one ingredient.

Business was so brisk that Lefty soon realized that he was going to need more space. He wanted to stay in Bernardston, but when space wasn't available in town he moved south to Greenfield

Beers Brewed: IPA, Pale Ale, English-Style Porter, Coffee Porter, Irish-Style Stout, Chocolate Oatmeal Stout.

The Pick: We're suckers for a good porter, and Lefty's English-Style Porter is a good, smooth-drinking example of the style.

and into an already crowded brewery territory; The People's Pint brew-pub is about a mile down the road. So far it seems to be serving Lefty well. His package brewery is doing brisk business and the added space has meant new, larger equipment.

Lefty is a new generation of American brewer. Having grown up with a wide selection of American craft beer available, he was inspired to first brew at home and did so for a decade, earning accolades from his neighbors, friends, and family. Buoyed by the praise, he was inspired to open his own shop. He quickly learned, however, that the transition from hobby to profession is one of toil.

"For the first six months, a hundred-hour work week was a short week," he said. And it wasn't just brewing. While girlfriend Melissa Forostoski works on a lot of the business side of things, Lefty found himself out selling the beer he made. Despite being situated in one of the more brew-fertile areas of the commonwealth, Lefty faced (and still does) an uphill battle against the larger, established brands like Bud and Miller.

His first break came in an unlikely place, the local VFW hall. "They had never seen anything like it," he said of the members. "They had a vote on if they should carry the beer and eventually did. They have tasted it and liked it, and these are tried and true Bud guys."

For now he is focusing on ales, with six variations available year-round, and working in a few seasonals. The ales produced are aimed at those seeking an introduction to craft beer. He is also pushing the pairing of food for all his beers, adding to their success.

Lefty is not only a passionate brewer, but an affable guy who is a lot of fun to hang out with, something visitors get to do when visiting the brewery for a sample and some swag. As far as new breweries go, Lefty's is all right.

Lefty's Brewing Company

Opened: 2010.
Owner: Bill Goldfarb.
Brewer: Bill Goldfarb.
System: 7-barrel brewhouse, 26-barrel cellar.
Production: 210 barrels in 2011.
Tours: Call the brewery for days and times.
Take-out beer: Available during tours, tastings. and events.
Special considerations: Handicapped-accessible.
Parking: Lot and street parking available.

Other area beer sites:
- **The Greenfield Grille** (30 Federal Street, Greenfield, 413-376-4777, www.the greenfieldgrille.com) is nearby and has some good craft selections on tap.
- **Hope and Olive** (44 Hope Street, Greenfield 413-774-3150, www.hopeand olive.com) has some good stuff on tap and a fun, hip atmosphere.

The People's Pint

24 Federal Street, Greenfield, MA 01301
413-773-0333 • www.thepeoplespint.com

For all you see at this cozy storefront brewpub, it's what you don't see that makes The People's Pint one of the most environmentally forward breweries in the country. Alden Booth is the owner of this establishment and subscribes to the philosophy that this is the only Earth we have, so it is best to take care of it. To that end, Booth has done everything he could possibly do to reduce the carbon and waste footprint of The People's Pint. "We'll have two hundred to three hundred people per day and we still only generate one bag of trash," he said with a deserved amount of pride.

The Pint orders food that is minimally packaged and refuses to have anything disposable—no plastic straws, no paper napkins. They compost every bit of organic waste from the tables. Anything that can be recycled is recycled. The food is contracted from local farms and the menu changes to reflect what's in season. Customers know that they won't be getting a tomato slice on hamburgers in the winter. In the beginning, Booth told us, things were difficult. Locals did not know what Swiss chard was, and selling customers on the garlic and kale quesadillas was a challenge.

Now more than fifteen years in, Booth is thankful that the local food movement has come into bloom. He now has access to local cheeses and dairy. Ice cream comes from a place up the street, and a roaster in town supplies coffee. The meat comes from local farms. Sodas are made from locally produced syrups.

Even some of the beers are locally sourced. When we visited, brewer Chris Sellers had just tapped his 100 percent Local Ale. Not only do we love the concept of this beer—all ingredients come from within a twenty-mile radius of the brewery—but it's well executed. Almost like an English mild, it has great malt flavor and a subtle hop finish.

We had scheduled an interview with Sellers and general manager Beth Fraser, but arrived a bit early. It was happy hour on a Friday and everyone had smiles on their faces. Getting down to work after ordering a sampler of beers, the concentration was broken when Bill the bartender asked if "kids like ice."

"I'm not going to put any in because I don't want to make it hard to get the drink out of the dachshund," he said, affixing the top of a child-size cup shaped like a long-snouted canine.

Within a few minutes it was clear to see that this was the neighborhood place, artistic yet humble. The staff knows the customers, their stories, and their kids' names. It's the kind of place where even first-time visitors feel at home. (Bill, by the way, asked that we refer to him in the book as "FlexMoneyClip," and who are we to say no?)

There is a lot to like about sitting at the Pint's thirteen-seat rounded bar. First, they have three beer engines! The chalkboard clearly displays what is on tap along with other libations, such as locally made ciders and meads. Here, customers can sit, order a ploughman's lunch or perhaps the pickled eggs, and enjoy the vintage bicycle posters on the walls.

We met up with Sellers and Fraser in the dining room and were treated to some delicious menu items. Don't come here expecting page after page of choices. But, know that no matter what you order, you'll be getting something delicious. From the sausage of the day to great Mexican burritos and quesadillas, it's all good.

Full but still thirsty, Sellers brought us to the brewery. When it first opened, the Pint's brewery was jammed into the basement underneath the bar; however, when some commercial space came available about a block away, Booth moved the operation over there. The move has allowed Sellers to really have a lot of fun. One of the first things that stood out on our tour was a Jack Daniel's barrel waiting to be filled with stout that would be aged for a few months.

Sellers is in his late twenties and has a passion that rivals the original American brewers, with a desire to make full-flavored beers that customers will be loyal to, find association with, and think about for

Beers Brewed: Natural Blonde Ale, Provider Pale Ale, Farmer Brown, Hope Street Bitter, Pied Piper IPA, Oatmeal Stout, Scotch Ale, Doppelbock, and a variety of seasonal and single-run beers.

The Pick: Easily the Pint's most anticipated seasonal offering, the Slippery Slope is a fruity, complex concoction of the braggart style. It combines local apple cider, honey, barley malt, and fresh ginger. This floral brew, as if descended from heaven, carries a wicked 9 percent alcohol content. At the brewery it is served in 12-ounce glasses, but 22-ounce bottles are available for at-home enjoyment.

just the right amount of time between swallows. The more we hung out, the more Sellers revealed his talents. He opened bottles of aged beers like his Russian Imperial Stout, creamy and heavy, full of booze, malt, chocolate, and deserving of awards. The main focus of the beers is English-style ales, and each of the year-round offerings from the blonde ale to the double IPA are distinct and bursting with flavor.

The brewery does its part to minimize waste as well, with spent grain going to local farms and to-go sales focused on reusable growlers.

As if there weren't already enough reasons to visit the Pint, there is a financial incentive as well. The Bike to Live program gives discounts to people who ride their bikes to the brewery. Since 2003, patrons have recorded around 50,000 miles and received nearly $3,000 in discounts.

"Our goal is to get people to realize that commuting by bike is more environmentally responsible, more enjoyable, physically healthier, less expensive, and often just as—or more—convenient as traveling by motorized vehicle," said Booth. "There is something magical about going places on your own power, at your own pace, on your own bicycle." And when that place is the Pint, pedal faster.

The People's Pint

Opened: 1997.
Owners: Alden Booth and Lissa Greenough.
Brewer: Chris Sellers.
System: 15-barrel pub.
Production: 950 barrels in 2011.
Hours: Daily, 11 A.M. to midnight.
Tours: By request only.
Take-out beer: 22-ounce bottles and growlers until 11 P.M.
Extras: Happy hour. Live music. If you ride your bike instead of driving your car, you get money off your bill at the restaurant.
Special considerations: Handicapped-accessible.
Parking: On street.
Other area beer sites:
  • **The Greenfield Grille** (30 Federal Street, Greenfield, 413-376-4777, www.the greenfieldgrille.com) is right next door to the brewery and has some good craft selections on tap.
  • **Hope and Olive** (44 Hope Street, Greenfield 413-774-3150, www.hopeand olive.com) has some good stuff on tap and a fun, hip atmosphere.

Paper City Brewery

108 Cabot Street, Holyoke, MA 01040
413-535-1588 • www.papercity.com

The sign outside Paper City blew away years ago during a storm, so first-time visitors might find it difficult to locate the brewery. As such, we navigated the trusty SUV through back alleys and along canals that house the strong brick factories that once made Holyoke a prosperous place.

When the brewery is located, however, the journey does not end at the banged-up green metal door. No, to get to the brewery, be prepared to climb five flights of stairs. After you catch your breath and those white spots fade from your vision, you're in the tasting room. A large, cavernous space bathed in light, it offers views of the valley and city that stretch for miles. Part saloon, part motorcycle museum and showcase for brewery collectibles, the room is also used for storage.

Jay Hebert is the owner and brewer at Paper City, and when the longtime homebrewer decided to open shop in 1995, he looked to one of his own buildings (he owns several in the area). "It has the hardest floor, the highest ceilings, and really makes for one of the most unique breweries out there," he said.

Indeed, when most breweries prefer to be on the ground, with brew kettles and fermentation tanks standing on poured concrete, Hebert put his hundreds of pounds of equipment on wide wooden beams that have stood up to the abuse of brewing, washing, and weight.

It likely helps that the building is no stranger to vice. It was at one time a tobacco warehouse (it also housed jackets made from alpaca wool, but that's less addictive), making it at least the second current brewery in the area to house smoking material. Berkshire Brewing Company is the other.

Originally Hebert planned to use the space for five years, but has settled in nicely. He is, of

Beers Brewed: Holyoke Dam Ale, Ireland Parish Golden Ale, India'n Pale Ale IPA, Riley's Stout, Winter Palace Wee Heavy, Cabot Street Summer Wheat, Heritage Red, Banchee Extra Pale Ale, Red Hat Razzberry, 1 Eared Monkey, P. C. Blue, Blonde Hop Monster, Winter Lager, Goat's Peak Bock, Summer Brew, Summer Time Pale Ale, Summit House Oktoberfest, Nut Brown.

The Pick: Their flagship, Ireland Parish Golden Ale, is a smooth, easy-drinking blonde with a subtle hop finish. Perfect for watching the game or hanging out with friends, it's a social beer and fits with the brewery's slogan: "tradition by the glass."

course, limited by weight, so expansion has been difficult, but Paper City continues to turn out plenty of beer: its own twenty varieties, as well as brews for several contract companies.

When he started brewing, Hebert favored English styles that relied heavily on malts and less on hops. He experimented with different styles over the years, but has remained mostly true to his brewing roots. He did fall on tough times after a rough deal with a distributor who buried the brand on shelves. To keep things going, Hebert used his extra space to contract out.

Currently they are brewing for High and Mighty, Rapscallion, and Landmark Beer of Syracuse and are also producing sodas and energy drinks. A freight elevator eases the job of getting ingredients up and bottles down.

Now, about those motorcycles we mentioned. They have a mix of vintage Harley-Davidson and classic Indian models that were made in nearby Springfield. Hebert fell in love with their workmanship, style, and history. He began collecting them, and when he moved the brewery to the new space, he figured it would be a good place to showcase them, rather than have them collect dust in a garage. "People really enjoy looking at them, learning more about them," he said.

Hebert sounded invigorated during a recent conversation. "We are looking to change things up a bit in a year from now and take more control of our destiny," he said. He's talking about an expanded line and "extreme" beers that are not necessarily big on alcohol, as well as Belgian-inspired beers and even lambics. He notes that in an older building, there are a lot of wild microbes that can be put to good use in those tart brews. He has even secured some wine barrels to start blending beers.

Even if it is difficult to find, it's time to visit Paper City. A map is included on the bottom of every six-pack sold, and Hebert said people who call will be guided in. "One of these days I'll get that sign back up," he said. "I just haven't had the chance yet."

Paper City Brewery

Opened: 1996.
Owner: Jay Herbert.
Brewers: Jay Herbert, Nicole Trano, and Shaun Rabzuik.
System: DME.
Production: 3,000 barrels in 2011.
Tours: Thursday and Friday in the afternoon. Call for times.
Take-out beer: Growlers

Extras: Live music on Fridays.

Special considerations: Handicapped–accessible.

Parking: Lot on site.

Other area beer sites:

- **Brennan's Place** (173 High Street, Holyoke, 413-533-9893) is a neighborhood joint in a somewhat rough part of the city. It's got decent beer selections, and provides an old-school setting to get a pint before moving on.

Element Brewing Company

30 Bridge Street, Millers Falls, MA 01349
413-835-6340 • www.elementbeer.com

Like a present waiting to be opened, each bottle of Element Brewing Company's beer comes wrapped in paper. It's thin tissue paper, the kind one tends to see around bottles of a certain foreign pedigree. It is an unusual presentation for an American brewery, but with so many offerings available on the shelf these days, newer operations need to do what they can to stand out. To the curious who take Element's offerings home comes a great reward.

The road to Element spans the history of several other Massachusetts breweries and shows the long friendship and partnership between three men: Dan Kramer, Tom Fields, and Ben Anhalt.

Kramer was the owner and brewer of the now-closed Maplewood Farms Brewery, a brewpub in Amherst. He hired Anhalt as an assistant and Fields was a regular who credits the two brewers with "getting a lot of people into good beer." When the brewery closed in 2004, Anhalt went to Paper City in Holyoke and Kramer wound up going to Opa-Opa in Southampton. Eventually, the two came together again with this new venture and brought in Fields, who serves as a catch-all; with his construction skills, he has helped keep things humming smoothly.

The brewery sits in a corner storefront that could just as easily be confused for a general store from the outside. It's one of many rehabbed build-

Beers Brewed: Extra Special Oak, Red Giant, Dark Element, and seasonal offerings.

The Pick: The 8-percent Red Giant has a complex hop aroma that dances with a sweetness given by caramel malts. It inspires, it comforts, and it lives up to its name.

ings that are getting a second life in this mill town that went bust decades ago. Kramer said they looked at a number of options before settling in Millers Falls. It helped that the local government was willing to work with them, that the storefront had the space needed, and that opening here meant being one of the only production breweries in the area. "It turned out to be a great spot," said Fields.

When they opened in 2009, they made a conscious decision to not open a brewpub, but rather focus on "quality products that are shelf-stable," explained Kramer. They also wanted to avoid going the same old six-pack route or make the styles people expect from a brewery. "We just did not want to make another IPA. There are already a hundred out there," said Kramer.

There are three flagship beers. American Black Ale, at 8.8 percent, has a smooth hop aroma and taste without dark malt bitterness or an overall boozy character. The Extra Special Oak, with flavors of toasted vanilla, spices, and wood, is delightfully smooth and full of character that reveals itself as the beer warms from being held in a snifter glass. Finally there is the Red Giant, a big ale that clocks in at 8 percent with robust hops. All three of their regular beers are ranked high on review sites, and after tasting, it is clear that each gets an extra boost of effervescence from bottle conditioning.

Another thing that helps Element's beer stand out is that each 750-milliliter bottle is finished with a cork and cage. Cork-finished bottles are a little taller than other bottles and there is something a bit more formal about them. There are only a handful of breweries that are using the packaging, but few deny that the bottles are more satisfying than a pry-off top. Cork-finished beers, like champagne and wine, open with a pop—an unmistakable sound that alerts the other senses and people in the room that something good is soon to come.

The experience is actually a little deeper than that though. Cork-finished bottles are a reminder to us all that beer comes from a place that has deep roots and shares more in common with wine than wine would like to admit. With the advent of metal bottle caps in the 1890s, many breweries abandoned corks for the newer, easier innovation in bottle sealing. This was readily seen, as it is today, among 12-ounce bottles. Cork-topped beers remained through the decades, but dwindled with the rising cost of equipment for the technology.

It is best to store cork-finished bottles standing up, not on their sides, as one would do with wine, said Ray Daniels, director of the Cicerone Certification Program. Wine needs some exposure to oxygen to mature and the corks help with that. "We are sure that is something not desirable for beer," he told us. "The ingress rate on cork-topped bottles is five to six times greater than a crown cap. That means the beer will mature far more rapidly." The corks, in essence, could potentially contaminate and spoil the beer. He also suggested that rather than keeping these bottles for the long haul, they are best consumed within a year and a half after leaving the brewery.

For Element, the philosophy is to make "artistic beers" that bring together art and science, said Kramer. When they thought of the beers that way, they began to really examine each part of the process, getting things down to basics, to the elements. That's where the name comes from. Like the packaging, Element truly is a gift.

Element Brewing Company

Opened: 2009.

Owners: Daniel Kramer, R. Ben Anhalt, and Tom Fields.

Brewers: Daniel Kramer and R. Ben Anhalt.

System: 4-barrel brewhouse, with two 4-barrel fermenters, two 15-barrel fermenters, four 4-barrel conditioning tanks, four 15-barrel conditioning tanks, one 4-barrel bright tank, and one 15-barrel bright tank.

Production: 300 barrels in 2011.

Tours: Offered by request during business hours, Monday, Thursday, Friday, and Saturday, noon to 6 P.M.

Take-out beer: Bottles.

Extras: Happy hour. Live music. Free tastings.

Special considerations: Handicapped-accessible.

Parking: Plenty of street parking.

Other area beer sites:

- **Miller's Pub** (25 East Main Street, Millers Falls, 413-659-3391) is directly across the street from Element and keeps all three of Element's year-round beers on tap.
- **Rendezvous** (78 3rd Street, Turners Falls, www.thevoo.net) has a good draft selection in a casual setting.

Barrington Brewery & Restaurant

420 Stockbridge Road, Great Barrington, MA 01230
413-528-8282 • www.barringtonbrewery.net

When the sun sits high in the southern sky over the Barrington Brewery, it means there is going to be plenty of the necessary hot water to use in the brewing process. Barrington boasts an impressive solar array on its roof that supplies heated water for the English-style beers brewed by Andrew Mankin, as well as for restaurant use. It's a deserved source of pride for Mankin and the brewery, and not a chance is missed to inform customers that they are drinking "solar-brewed beer" with "sun power in every glass."

The oversized barrel that greets visitors as they pull into the gravel parking lot is a clear indication that beer is indeed here. By the entrance, a yellow diamond traffic sign proclaiming "Beer Crossing" is a good indication as well. The building itself—yellow paint, maroon trim—looks like a hiking lodge or a really well-lived-in and loved larger house.

Once inside, it's clear to see that this is a comfortable restaurant. Large windows looking out to a patio area give the space a cozy but bright feel. Inside the pub area, the smallish wooden bar is jammed with regulars. Given the proximity, conversation flows freely between patrons. Low ceilings, vintage beer coasters on the wall, and ancient bottles on a shelf give the feeling that Barrington has been around far longer than 1995.

Mankin, who was an avid homebrewer, furthered his career with an apprenticeship at Vaux Brewing in England, where he learned the nuances and tradition of crafting ales. When Gary Happ, a local bar owner, came knocking in the early 1990s with the plan to open a brewpub, Mankin could not refuse and a partnership was formed.

Mankin, an affable fellow, recounted the story to us while sitting at the bar, an Old World–style spot, with a traditional cash register that punches the air with an old-fashioned cha-ching each time a sale is rung up. It's several steps from the raised

Beers Brewed: Ice Glenn IPA, Black Bear Stout, Barrington Brown, Hopland Pale Ale, Berkshire Blonde, Raspberry Ale, Vienna, Firecracker Imperial IPA, Mankin's English Ale, Wedded Bliss, Bavarian Wheat, E.S.B., Porter, Prague Pilsner, Scottish Ale, Yule Fuel, Alt, "R" Hop, Mankin's Organic.

The Pick: The Barrington Brown is a full-bodied English-style ale, with a medium roast but deep flavor.

brewhouse, a wood-paneled kettle and mash tun, with fermenters and bright tanks below.

From this setup Mankin produces a variety of beers and there is always a generous amount on tap. When we visited in the fall, there was an Oktoberfest and a floral fresh hop available. At the rate we watched pints poured, customers were clearly getting their fill and coming back for more.

Education plays a big part. The Barrington staff is well-versed in both the brewing process and the beers on tap. There are still a lot of first-time customers who walk through the door and expect to get a familiar brand in a bottle. The staff can point them to a beer that is similar and bring about a new convert.

It's also important to note that Barrington has a great kitchen. Chicken pot pie, ribs, and sea scallops are all served in generous and tasty portions. Sandwiches like the brewer's pocket (spinach, smoked turkey, bacon, sprouts, onions, bleu cheese dressing, and melted Swiss on pita bread) are worth a spot in a regular rotation. Their chocolate stout cake is incredible. All baking, by the way, is done on the premises. "We are really proud of our kitchen," Mankin told us.

He's also really proud of those solar panels. While generally an environmentally conscious lot, brewers in this area of the state seemingly take it more serious than others. Mankin wanted to make sure the brewery was doing its part, so in 2007 they installed the thirty panels on the roof, which provide a thousand gallons of hot water on a daily basis. "It's about looking at the big picture," said Mankin.

Adding to the picture is a large banquet room they built a few years ago. Attached to the brewery via the kitchen, Crissey Farm Berkshire Banquet House is a large, welcoming space that hosts weddings, fundraisers, and other parties. It is also home to the local Episcopal church on Sunday mornings. When the congregation's original building was deemed structurally unsound, Mankin and Happ stepped up and offered the space for weekly worship. It's led to some interesting scenarios. What might be the scene of a raucous party the night before, with shots and pints flowing freely, turns solemn just a few hours later.

One great feature of the space is a view of Monument Mountain, one of the most popular in the Berkshires. It was on that terrain that Herman Melville is said to have cultivated his idea for *Moby Dick*. He would traverse the mountain with friends Nathaniel Hawthorne and Oliver Wendell Holmes, where it's likely a few drinks were consumed along the way. Now, hikers and campers have Barrington Brewery to ply them with pints and inspiration after a day on the mountain.

Barrington Brewery & Restaurant

Opened: 1995.

Owners: Andrew Mankin and Gary Happ.

Brewers: Andrew Mankin, Scott Craumer, and Dave Toomey.

System: 7-barrel.

Production: 1,100 barrels in 2011.

Hours: Opens daily at 11:30 A.M. Kitchen closes at 9:30 P.M. Monday through Thursday, 10 P.M. Friday and Saturday, and 9 P.M. Sunday.

Take-out beer: Growlers, 22-ounce bottles, and kegs.

Special considerations: Handicapped-accessible.

Parking: On site.

Other area beer sites:

- **The Route 7 Grill** (999 Main Street, Great Barrington, 413-528-3235, www.route 7grill.com) is a wonderful farm-to-table restaurant, with a decent craft beer list and some of the best pork dishes you'll find anywhere.

Northampton Brewery Bar + Grille

13 Old South Street, Northampton, MA 01060
413-584-9903 • www.northamptonbrewery.com

There is no doubt that Janet Egelston has left an indelible mark on the American brewing scene. Following a trip to Santa Cruz, California, in the mid-1980s, she was introduced to the brewpub concept. Intrigued and inspired, she partnered with Mark Metzger and her brother, Peter, who was homebrewing at the time, and returned to Northampton, an artistic city where her mother grew up.

The trio opened their doors in 1987, becoming the second brewpub in the state (behind the now-closed Commonwealth Brewing Company in Boston), and have been blessed with success ever since. Now heralded as the oldest brewpub in New England, Northampton shows no sign of slowing down.

Northampton has gone through a few incarnations. The old carriage house had been turned into an office space. The Egelston siblings added a kitchen, bar, and brewing equipment. They opened an outdoor space a year later, followed by a major expansion in 1995. This allowed for a larger kitchen and a 150-seat rooftop space with its own bar.

With its light wood accents and earth tones, it now has a modern coffee shop feel. It's a comfortable place that encourages lingering conversations over the course of a few pints. "Expect to be welcomed and treated well," said Janet. "We've put a lot of thought into the bewery, a lot of care into training staff, a lot of care into the beer and food."

So let's talk about the beer. With only a 10-barrel brewhouse, Northampton turns out a dizzying array of beers, and each one is worthy of your time and taste buds. The bitter has hints of apple; the porter has a kiss of smoke. The beers, one after another, reveal new flavors with each swallow. Their pale and India pale ales make the most of the hops they have. There are seasonals that draw inspiration from Germany, Belgium, and across the states. Where some brewpubs have the bad habit of turning out beers that look different shades but taste the same, Northampton runs the gamut of flavor.

Following their success in Northampton, the Egelston siblings (Metzger left the partnership after several years) set their sights north. In 1991, they opened the Portsmouth Brewery in Portsmouth, New Hampshire. Three years later they opened another brewery in Portsmouth, this one named Smuttynose. With inventive, flavorful beers that have a loyal following and new lifelong fans arriving all the time, the trio of breweries was a formidable force and constant winner of medals.

In 2000, Janet and Peter bought each other out of the businesses, with Janet retaining ownership of Northampton and Peter taking Portsmouth and keeping a majority stake in Smuttynose. They remain happy siblings, and there is often Smuttynose on tap at the pub.

"It was a great partnership, but I just wanted to be in one location," said Janet. Staying put in Northampton has allowed her to explore new avenues for the brewery, including partnering with J.O.E.'s Farm, a produce provider just ten miles from the kitchen. Thanks to a greenhouse, the brewery gets fresh veggies all year long.

Beers Brewed: Shovel ESB, Altbier, Black Cat Stout, Byzantine Blonde, Daniel Shays Best Bitter, Golden Lager, Hefe-Weizenheimer, Hoover's Porter, Nonotuk IPA, Northampton Pale Ale, Old Brown Dog, Paradise City Gold, Redheaded Stepchild, Unquamonk Amber Lager, Windbreaker Hefeweizen, and a variety of seasonal offerings and single-batch brews.

The Pick: Blue Boots IPA. This India pale ale is light in color, strong in body, and mouth-puckeringly bitter. Three grains and four types of hops make this unfiltered ale complex. And when it's available go for the Black Boots, or what they call the "evil twin" of Blue Boots. It's a black IPA with nice malt characteristics, but a big punch of hops.

The commitment to local business and the environment extends beyond just the plate. The kitchen was recently retrofitted to energy-saving appliances, cutting utility bills in half. There is also an aggressive recycling program at the brewery.

Northampton is a town that appreciates arts and creativity. The brewery has become a cultural hub over the years, as well as a welcome respite during the icy grip of New England winters. On a recent visit, we had the pleasure of watching ruddy, pink-cheeked customers walk through the front door, as they peeled off layers and basked in the warmth of the welcoming atmosphere, quickly settling in as if they were home. The same was true in visits during warmer months, when the sounds of conversations drift from the rooftop and the brewery adds more life to this lively town.

That visit to California a quarter century ago led to one of the best brewpubs in the East. All vacations should go so well.

Northampton Brewery Bar + Grille

Opened: 1987.

Owner: Janet Egelston.

Brewers: Donald Pacher and assistant Steven Bilodeau.

System: JV Northwest 10-barrel direct-fire brewhouse, with two 10-barrel fermenters, two 20-barrel fermenters, and one 30-barrel fermenter.

Production: 900 barrels in 2011.

Hours: Monday through Saturday, 11:30 A.M. to 12:30 A.M.; Sunday, noon to 12:30 A.M.

Tours: By appointment.

Take-out beer: Growlers

Extras: Outdoor dining. Beer socials. Live Irish music on Sunday from 3 P.M. to 6 P.M.

Special considerations: Handicapped-accessible.

Parking: Garage on one side and parking lot on the other.

Other area beer sites:

- **Sierra Grille** (41 Strong Ave. #A, Northampton, 413-584-1150, www.sierra grille.net) has a great draft list and killer food.

Opa-Opa Steakhouse & Brewery

169 College Highway, Southampton, MA 01073
413-527-0808 • www.opaopasteakhousebrewery.com

The ceramic plate hits the floor with a satisfying crash and the crowd simultaneously screams out "OPA!" followed by claps and cheers. It's a charity night at Opa-Opa Steakhouse & Brewery, a cowboy-themed family restaurant, and after getting bids that will be donated to a worthy cause, the "celebrity" bartender gets to smash a plate in the true Greek tradition. Everyone except the clean-up crew wins, and it adds to the overall eclectic nature of this place.

This brewpub is the realization of a dream that some Greek fellows had years ago. They left their native land, wound up in Western Massachusetts, and got to work building their own American dream. In a way, it's a traditional pioneer story of people going west to find their fortune, to make a better life. Fortunately for us, that dream included red meat and beer.

And as much as this is a brewpub, it is also a saloon. Take for example the Texas-sized lacquered bar, featuring classic shots of ranchers playing cards and various winning poker hands encased underneath. Country music plays from above. Servers are clad in denim and sport red kerchiefs around their necks. The whole thing has a comfortable, yet throwback feel.

It's also about family. There are both Kodak and Polaroid prints tacked to the walls featuring the scores of customers who have passed through the doors celebrating birthdays and anniversaries or just spending regular nights there—moments that weave the tapestry of life.

"We're loud, it gets crazy in here, it's to be encouraged," explained cofounder Tony Rizos. When we visited, the noise was manageable, but people were clearly enjoying their evening out.

Like its sister restaurant-brewery, the Brewmaster's Tavern, Opa-Opa has its own set of rules, although some are contradictory:

- All guests or patrons who refuse to tap a toe or scoot their boots on the dance floor shall be asked to change their attitude.

Beers Brewed: Opa Opa Light, Kix Brew, Opa American Wheat, Porter, Red Rock Amber, Raspberry Wheat, Honesty 47 Pale Ale, Buckwheat IPA, Opa Opa Brown Ale.

The Pick: Served cold, Honesty 47 Pale Ale has a pleasing hop bitterness. It goes well with just about everything on the menu and is perfect by itself, partner.

- Dancing with horses, dogs, coyotes, and lampshades is not to be encouraged.
- No guests of Opa-Opa, or any hired hand (except the trail boss), is permitted to carry on or about his or her person or in his or her saddle bags, any pistol, dirk, dagger, sling shot, knuckles, bowie knife or other similar instruments for shootin' or fightin'.
- Please leave your wallets, money belts and cash at the door with the trail boss. Thank you.
- If lead starts flyin' in here, grab your plate and eat under the table. It'll stop in a minute.

Honestly, there have been no reports of gunplay in the brewery's history, but the rules are enough to give a patron a slight grin and ease into the generous plates and pints.

"When we came here we worked hard, really hard," said Rizos. "We had a little bit of luck as well." The idea for a cowboy-themed steakhouse was his, but it is one of the other owners who gets the full treatment in a large oil painting in the bar area depicting him in a black Stetson and bolo tie.

Like any good Greek restaurant there is ouzo, twelve varieties to be exact. The anise-flavored liquor makes for a great chaser after a pint of one of the many varieties of beer Opa-Opa makes and serves. There are varieties from the palest of ales to a double IPA and everything in between. Opa-Opa has a 7-barrel brewhouse at the far end of the bar, and brewer Dennis Bates still uses it for test batches and smaller runs, but most of the beer is made down the road at their newer, larger facility attached to the Brewmaster's Tavern.

As for the phrase "opa-opa," it is a term that is used to convey a feeling of great joy and jubilation. Spend a night at this place and you'll be saying it yourself.

Opa-Opa Steakhouse & Brewery

Opened: 2004.

Owners: Themis and Tony Rizos.

Brewer: Dennis Bates.

System: 7-barrel CM Brewhouse.

Production: N/A.

Hours: Restaurant open Monday through Thursday 11 A.M. to 10 P.M.; Friday and Saturday, 11 A.M. to 11 P.M.; and Sunday, 11 A.M. to 10 P.M. Bar open Monday through Thursday, 11 A.M. to midnight; Friday and Saturday, 11 A.M. to 1 A.M.; and Sunday, 11 A.M. to midnight.

Tours: By appointment.

Take-out beer: Growlers.

Extras: Occasional events, live music.

Special considerations: Handicapped-accessible.

Parking: On-site lot.

Berkshire Brewing Company

12 Railroad Street, South Deerfield, MA 01373
(413) 665-6600, www.berkshirebrewingcompany.com

"Welcome to the wonderful world of Berkshire," said Gary Bogoff, channeling his inner Willy Wonka as he opened the door from his brewery's laboratory onto the brewing floor. What became immediately clear was that the Berkshire Brewing Company knows how to maximize the space it has.

"We have just six thousand square feet of space, but we filled it up quite nicely," said Bogoff with a smile. "It was never meant to be a brewery, but works well. We've stuffed a lot of stuff in."

While it might seem a little disjointed at first, one quickly sees that everything is perfectly thought out (and wedged in), so that from grain to garage, there is a logical flow to the space. There is also a hodgepodge of equipment, like the soda syrup mixing tank that is now a mash tun, the old 60-barrel fermenters from a long-closed Pabst brewery in New Jersey, and repurposed dairy equipment used as bright tanks.

One does not have to finish their first 22-ounce bottle of a Berkshire brew to know that they have stumbled across something special. From the Dean's Beans Coffeehouse Porter, which is a perfect way to start the day, to the Steel Rail Extra Pale Ale, which beer writer Lew Bryson described as "what the water in heaven oughta taste like," Berkshire does not make a bad beer. They don't even make a mediocre beer, an all right beer, or

Beers Brewed: Steel Rail E.P.A., Berkshire Traditional Pale Ale, Drayman's Porter, Lost Sailor I.P.A., Dean's Beans Coffeehouse Porter, Shabadoo Black & Tan, Russian Imperial Stout, River Ale, Gold Spike German-Style Kolsch, and specialty and seasonal offerings.

The Pick: River Ale is a perfect balance of malt and a single hop—Willamette—that gives a sweet flavor with a nutty aroma and a slight prick of spice. This 7 percent is perfect any time of year.

one that is simply okay. No, they consistently make great beer. This is beer that is sought after from around the country, beer that is stocked up when people come through the area so they can take it back home and enjoy it there.

Bogoff knows people drive from far and wide for the beers and said that he's often asked to grow his distribution network. But he has taken the "pebble in the center of the pond" philosophy. That means Berkshire will make sure demand is met in the areas closest to the brewery first and will grow out from there as production and customer demands permit.

Berkshire's beers are unfiltered, unpasteurized, and contain no chemical additives or preservatives. They're bottled cold, stored cold, and then shipped inside refrigerated trucks owned by the brewery to chilled display cases in stores. The distributors who get the beer into Vermont and New Hampshire take the same care with the beer as the Berkshire guys do. "Three hours is as far as you can go from the brewery and still find us," Bogoff said.

His business card calls him the CEO, treasurer, and brewer, but spend a day with Bogoff walking around the brewery and you'll see a true tradesman at work. He fixes equipment, monitors shipments, and pitches in on the keg line, all while talking about the beers that made his brewery one of the most respected in the East.

And like most breweries of its generation, it started with a modest plan by two friends to make some good beer. It was 1992 when Bogoff and Chris Lalli decided that their passion for fresh ale was more than a hobby and needed to become a business. They worked on a plan, secured this location (once a cigar factory), and opened for business in the summer of 1994. With beer this good, word spread quickly and the orders soon came pouring in from draft accounts. Soon enough they gave the people what they wanted and began to fill those 22-ounce bomber bottles and growlers. In the early days, the task of filling those vessels relied on a dedicated group of volunteers.

One of them was named Dick Schatz, who along with two pals, Fran Lemay and Butch Denofrio, arrived each week to bottle, cap, and label. Before he died in 2006, Schatz, a World War II veteran, bequeathed his impressive and expansive collection of beer signs from around the world to Berkshire Brewing. These clocks, mirrors, neon signs, and pool table lamps are the tapestry of the brewery tasting room, named in Schatz's honor.

That's where we spoke at length with Bogoff and realized his passion for no-frills but flavorful beers and learned about the brewery's commitment to the people who drink their wares. "It's all about the beer, but beer is nothing without the people," said Bogoff, repeating the company motto.

Our tour completed, Bogoff opened the brewery door to the parking lot and was met with a long line of people—the next lucky ones to visit the wonderful world of Berkshire.

Berkshire Brewing Company

Opened: 1994.

Owners: Gary Bogoff and Chris Lalli.

Brewers: Gary Bogoff, Chris Lalli, and six additional brewers.

System: Custom-built 20-barrel brewhouse, the combination of many different systems from several different industries.

Production: 30,000 barrels capacity. 22,000 barrels in 2011.

Tours: Saturday at 1 P.M.

Take-out beer: Not available.

Special considerations: Handicapped-accessible.

Parking: On site.

Other area beer sites:

- **Champney's Restaurant and Tavern at the Deerfield Inn** (81 Main Street, Deerfield, 413-774-5587, www.champneysrestaurant.com/tavern) has a cozy bar, which not only serves BBC beers but those from a local kid who made a name for himself in the brewing industry, Sam Calagione of Dogfish Head in Delaware.

The Brewmaster's Tavern

4 Main Street, Williamsburg, MA 01096
413-268 7741 • www.thebrewmasterstavern.com

On the front page of the Brewmaster's Tavern menu is a list of rules. Number 17 states, "Smile. A pleasant smile is pleasing to behold." Settling into the comfortable U-shaped wood bar, we found it difficult not to smile. There, at the front of the bar, were twenty-four taps of Opa-Opa beer, along with one tap for a frothy and robust root beer.

Although it dates back to 1812 and was rebuilt in 1873 following a devastating fire, this restaurant, formerly a hotel and then a livery store, has today a decidedly Colonial feel. Yet its large rooms are bathed in natural light from windows in the dining room, and there is vintage beer paraphernalia on the walls. What can we say? It works.

The same goes for the kitchen, where they are turning out hearty portions of everything from boiled New England dinners consisting of corned beef, potato, cabbage, and carrots to grilled pork tenderloin or complete turkey dinners. The sandwiches are guaranteed to leave you stuffed as well, but save room for the beer. Like we said, there are a lot of choices.

"We're just trying to make the best beer we can," said Dennis Bates, the head brewer. "And we want to give people a lot of choice." So on any given day a thirsty customer can go from the double IPA to the house lager to the dark wheat beer over to the English-style porter.

Dennis told us that fruit-tinged beers are especially popular with customers, and so the brewery staff releases flavors like apricot, blueberry, raspberry, and blackberry. They typically use extracts to flavor the beer, but mercifully they have an easy hand, so that the flavor is subtler than some other syruplike fruit ales and lagers on the market.

We chatted a while with Dennis about his background. He started working at sister restaurant Opa Opa and became the assistant brewer under Dan Kramer (now of Element Brewing) and later moved into the main spot. After some conversation, and still not making it halfway through the house beers, Dennis invited us back to the brewery.

The piece of property that the tavern sits on came with some additional land, and the owners wanted to install a full commercial brewery where they could have better control over the brewing process and their bottling line. Until the building's four-thousand-square-foot brewery opened in 2007, the beers were produced at the 7-barrel brewhouse at the Opa Opa Steakhouse and Brewery, about a twenty-five-minute ride away in Southampton, or produced at the Olde Saratoga contract brewery in New York.

Limited by the footprint the building could hold, there wasn't the space to build out, so they built up. From the outside, the four-story brewery matches the restaurant with its red painted wood sides and large windows. Only the two large grain silos give away what lies inside.

Dennis nimbly climbed metal stairs, worked his way around the equipment while giving a tour (we were joined by a few avid homebrewers who had a ton of technical questions and dreams of their own

Beers Brewed: Opa Opa Lager, Blueberry Lager, Watermelon Ale, F-15 Eagle, Double IPA, King Oar Oatmeal Stout, Southampton Porter, Blackberry Brown, Red Rock Light.

The Pick: The Southampton Porter is malty, rich, and perfectly quaffable.

breweries dancing in their eyes), and showed both his affable nature and respect for the beer.

This is where they bottle the Opa-Opa beers, and the brewhouse has the ability to crank out an impressive twelve thousand barrels per year. They have already flooded the market with five thousand barrels, and the owners are looking to increase distribution. Good news for those who like choices.

After the tour, it is worth spending some time in their recently constructed beer garden area—picnic tables under some shade on the side of the brewery building. There, one can contemplate the other rules of his brewery tavern.

Number seven states, "Associate yourself with Men of good Quality if you Esteem your own Reputation; for 'tis better to be alone than in bad Company."

Look around, those people sitting around you enjoying locally made beer are certainly those of quality. Good choice.

The Brewmaster's Tavern

Opened: 2007.

Owners: Themis and Tony Rizos.

Brewer: Dennis Bates.

System: N/A

Production: N/A

Hours: Monday through Friday, 11 A.M. to 11 P.M.; Saturday 10 A.M. to 11 P.M.; and Sunday 7 A.M. to 11 P.M.

Tours: Saturdays at 2:30 P.M.

Take-out beer: Growlers.

Special considerations: Handicapped-accessible.

Parking: On-site lot.

Wandering Star Craft Brewery

Pittsfield, Mass.

11 Gifford Street, Pittsfield, MA
917-573-3942 • www.wanderingstarbrewing.com

There are likely very few breweries in this country that are obligated by their insurance company to guard against terrorism. For Wandering Star in Pittsfield, located a stone's throw away from the General Dynamics bomb-making facility, it's not only necessary but important.

This is a distance away from where Chris Post wanted to be when he first hatched the idea to open a brewery in Western Massachusetts about a decade ago. Post hailed from southern England, immigrated to New York City in 1996, and soon enough found himself spending weekends in the Berkshires. He fell for the town of North Adams, in the most northwestern part of the state, and came up with the idea of a brewery called Nomad (NOrth Massachusetts ADams). But logistical issues with a building and a "very polite" letter from a pub in Wisconsin with a similar name scuttled those plans.

It was a happy coincidence, however, because the day the North Adams plans fell through Post was driving through Pittsfield, near the bomb factory, when he saw a For Sale sign.

"People still refer to the building as Rayner's Auto Parts," said Post when we visited. The barnlike structure with large bay doors on either end is conducive to the automotive industry, but works perfectly fine as a brewery.

The centerpiece is a copper-clad 15-barrel DME system that Post found on eBay back in 2004. At the time he was working in finance in Manhattan, but had been bitten by the brewery bug and was harboring aspirations of one day opening his own place. So, idly searching the Internet, he happened upon this full brewpub system from the Lighthouse Depot in Michigan, which had been forced out of business by unscrupulous politicians. Three days later, Post was still the only bidder, got the system, and found himself in the Great Lakes State

Beers Brewed: Mild At Heart English Dark Mild Ale, Alpha Pale, Raindrop Pale Ale, Berkshire Hills 01021 Saison, Bash-Bish-Bock, Bert's Disqualified Imperial Stout, Zingari Belgian Witbier.

The Pick: Post's Zingari Belgian Witbier with lemon grass, cardamom, and fenugreek has a sweet, floral aroma with great depth. Still, it remains light, drinkable, and completely refreshing.

moving the system into storage. There it would sit for a few years until he finally transferred it to North Adams.

Meanwhile Post continued to work in finance, met his wife Shannon (the CEO of the brewery), and together they had two boys. When the Great Recession came about, Post first found himself out of a city job and working in Albany. Soon he found the motivation—or push—from his bosses to strike out on his own, leave finance behind, and become a full-time brewer.

The good news, which is reflected in his lineup of beers, is that Post had been practicing all along. When living in New York City, he took a number of brewing classes, talked with brewers and hung out with experts like Michael Jackson when they visited the city. He eventually landed an internship at Chelsea Brewing on the city's West Side. From there he went to Greenpoint Brewing on Long Island and learned the ins and outs of working in a large brewery.

Post acted on the For Sale sign in Pittsfield and soon found a home for his unattached brewing system. Connected and impressive, it is now tended to by Post on a daily basis, played on by his two sons, and guarded at night by an affectionate calico cat named Fuggles, who also keeps an eye on the grain for any critters who are looking for a snack.

This draft-only brewery has become a gathering place for the area since the last brewery went out of business a few years ago. Post, knowing the importance of beer to the local community, made his first batch as Wandering Star on National Homebrew Day in 2011, inviting the local homebrewers to come down with their own rigs and join in the fun.

He quickly learned the nuances of his system, and between auger jams and flow problems added on a few extra hours to the brew day. The result has been impressive. He's currently making six beers and has given them a definitive personal twist that demands a closer examination and quick praise.

Post has partnered with two of New York City's great beer men on this venture. The first is Chris Cuzme, a homebrewing legend in the city, advocate for good beer, stellar musician, and all-around good guy. The second is Alex Hall, a cask beer expert and brewer. Over the last several years, Hall has worked tirelessly to raise the profile of Real Ale in a city that doesn't always appreciate beer.

When most think of cask ale, they will cite "lack of carbonation" or how the beer is flat. In reality, that's not the case. "If kept correctly, there is a subtle, natural carbonation, which imparts a gentle gas prickle on the tongue, as opposed to a harsh one from CO_2-pushed beer. The implication that cask beer is meant to be flat is incorrect and is damaging to the growth of beer as such in its most natural form of dispense," Hall said.

Hall joined others in saying that aggressive, extraneous gas in a beer can take away from the full mouthfeel; however, cask beer does not fall on the other extreme of the spectrum by being considered flat or near flat.

Also, linked with this issue is the serving temperature of modern kegged beer. To taste beer to the full flavor spectrum possible, traditional cellar temperature (54 to 56 degrees F.) is optimum. The temperature is, yes, warmer than the freezing mark that some American breweries say is necessary to drink their beers. Serving a beer at the proper cellar temperature allows for a greater aroma from the beer, a more accurate mouthfeel and a still thirst-quenching beverage.

"Chilled any further, nuances on the palate are lost," said Hall. "Cask beer is ideally served at that temperature, so the joint issue of this and the gentle carbonation from the secondary fermentation in the cask are jointly vital for the full flavor spectrum to be enjoyed."

The common fallacy, Hall concluded, that cask beer is "warm and flat" must not be continued. "Any beer that is truly warm and flat would be undrinkable," said Hall. "Cask beer in good condition with a gentle, naturally produced carbonation is many miles away from that description."

Post said that Wandering Star will continue to put their beer in casks, but will be very selective as to where they are served. He noted Hall's information on cask beer and said it was not worth having the beer spoil if it sat around unused for several days.

Like so many others in his generation of brewers, Post sees each day as a gift. "I don't want to do anything else in the world."

Wandering Star Craft Brewery

Opened: 2011.
Owners: Chris and Shannon Post.
Brewers: Chris Post.
System: DME 15-barrel single infusion.
Production: 1,000 barrels in 2011.
Tours: By appointment only.
Take-out beer: None currently available.
Special considerations: Handicapped-accessible.
Parking: Onsite lot.

Other area beer sites:

- **Moe's Tavern** (10 Railroad Street, Lee, 413-243-6637) has an inspired tap list, a friendly owner, a great selection of scotch, and some tasty wings. It's worth multiple visits.

- **Purple Pub** (65 Spring Street, Williamstown, 413-458-0095) is to be lauded for its commitment to local beer served well in a comfortable atmosphere.

- **Hops and Wines Beer Garden and Brasserie** (16 Water Street, Williamstown, 413-884-1372, www.hopsandvinesma.com) is nearby and offers both casual and formal dining with well-thought-out beer and wine lists. Reservations are recommended.

- **Old Forge Restaurant** (125 North Main Street, Lanesboro, 413-442-6797) will require a visit of a few hours to give their beer selection the attention it deserves. Also, save room for a burger.

Beer Styles

Beer falls into two overall styles: ales and lagers. Yeast is the key difference here. In the case of lagers, the yeast that is used gathers during fermentation at the bottom of the tank. With ales, it gathers towards the top. Another factor is timing and temperature. Ales age for just a few weeks, at around 40 to 55 degrees Fahrenheit, while lagers can age for months at around the freezing mark to 45 degrees.

Bryce Eddings, who writes about beer for About.com, puts it this way: "Although both are beer, the two are as different as red and white wines. Lagers are clean, refreshing beers with typically light aroma and flavor. They are invariably served cold and can pair easily with a wide variety of food. Ales are complex, flavorful beers. Many are served closer to room temperature and contain rich aroma and flavor. Their complexity makes pairing a more selective, but highly rewarding, task."

There are varying degrees within every category, but by knowing these basic styles you will be able to learn what you like and dislike and order with some confidence when you walk into a place that offers more than thirty taps.

Let's start with lagers. Chances are it's the category you're most likely to see advertised on television, because it's a style favored by the big breweries. These tend to be thirst-quenching beers, subtle on both malt and hop flavors. The light and regular varieties (think Budweiser) often use corn and rice as ingredients.

There is a wide assortment of lagers, with variations in color and flavor. On the lighter side are *pilsners*, such as Bohemian pilsner (Pilsner Urquell), German pilsner (Victory Prima Pils), and Dortmunder Export (DAB Export). These usually fall into the 4- to 5-percent ABV range. *Ambers* have a heavy malt emphasis. Types include Oktoberfest, Märzen, Vienna lager, and amber American lager. These typically fall into the high 4- to 6-percent ABV range. *Dark lagers*, such as Munich dunkel or shwarzbier, are roastier and more complex, ranging between 4.2 and 6.0 ABV. Finally there are *bocks*, such as maibock or dopplebock, that are strong, hearty, and often a little sweet. Some of these are as high as 8 percent ABV.

German variations of light or pale lagers are known as *helles*, and traditional brews follow the *Reinheitsgebot*, or German Purity Law, which allows beer to be made with just water, malt, hops, and yeast. One example of a helles is the Weihenstephaner original. An option that's a bit darker is *dunkel*, which has a nice sweetness and hopefully notes of dessert flavors like chocolate or toffee (Dinkel Acker Dark). German lagers can also come and go with the seasons; maibock, a hearty spring beer, usually appears in February and March to welcome warmer weather (Victory St. Boisterous), while the Oktoberfest beers lead us into fall.

For ales, ease in with a Kölsch, cream ale, or blonde ale. These light and refreshing beers usually carry a bit more flavor than the light lagers and pilsners, but are built to be consumed without loading you down.

Even in the depths of dive bars it's now common to see *pale ales* on tap. These moderately hopped brews are made with any variety of hops and offer a nice bitter flavor to balance out the malt. Usually good for a few rounds without killing taste buds, pale ales (Sierra Nevada Pale Ale, Deschutes Mirror Pond) are great year-round but very pleasant in warmer weather.

An India pale ale, or IPA, especially those made in the United States, will be more aggressive on the hops, with brewers working to get the bitterness units up to a tangy delight. Even more aggressive are the Imperial IPAs, which push the limits of hops to the brink of chewiness and powerful aromas (Pliny the Elder, Dogfish Head 120 Minute IPA).

There are red ales, amber ales, and brown ales. So much depends on what the brewer used as malt (for color) and hops (for flavor), and no two are exactly alike. Many places now offer sample trays, and if you prefer ales, this is a good way to find something you like.

For *stout*, Guinness is the most likely to be found on tap, but there are others that can be found in this ale style that use dark, roasted malts for a flavor profile that can conjure up notes of coffee, espresso, chocolate, caramel, and even dark fruit, depending on the style. Guinness is an example of a dry stout but other stout variations include sweet, oatmeal, milk, foreign extra, and Russian imperial.

Similar to a stout is *porter*. Also an ale, it is usually found behind the bar as a brown porter (Fuller's), but can also be robust (Bell's porter) or in the Baltic variety (Southampton Imperial Baltic Porter), where deep licorice notes with ABV pushing 10 percent may be found.

As we settle into cooler months, check out strong ales. These can be old ale, barley wine or Wee Heavy; all are quite boozy, with hefty malt and hop balance.

Up to this point, we've focused on German and American styles. One famed brewing country that should not be overlooked is Belgium, home to Trappist monasteries that make some of the world's finest beer. You're most likely to see these beers in bottles, but will occasionally see some on draft.

Belgian beers include *witbier*, a hazy wheat-heavy brew with spicy notes; *Belgian pale ale*, which has more of a malt profile and some fruit notes; and *saison*, a wonderful beer that has its origins in the fields, where it was fed to workers to help fortify them for an afternoon of toil, and has earthy notes, full but refreshing. There is the *Biere de Garde*, a beer with a woodsy, cellar-like character that comes with proper aging and offers a dry flavor and finish.

Keep in mind that this is just a rough guide and that in some bars you might see something we didn't touch on here. Don't be deterred! Ask your bartender or server about the brew in question. The same goes for someone next to you at the bar nursing that different-looking beer. Ask for a sample and see if you like it. It's okay to experiment. By exploring the many flavors of beer you will learn to appreciate new styles, further your own brew education, and be able to order each pint with confidence.

Once you've chosen your beer, it's important to make sure you have the correct vessel. The United States has not been as quick to embrace proper glassware as other countries, like Germany and Belgium. Here, we usually get the standard 16-ounce shaker pint. But a proper glass enhances aromas and flavors. Try a snifter for that barley wine, a stemmed goblet for that Abbey Dubbel, a larger tulip glass for a saison or Flemish Red, a pilsner glass for a Kolsch or cream ale, and an Irish imperial pint for a stout.

Do not be afraid to ask questions. Your brewers and bartenders are likely affable folks who are eager to talk about their craft. If you have a question, they will likely have correct answers or at least know someone who will. Read books about beer and brewing, and check out regular periodicals like *Ale Street News* and the many websites that are devoted to all things beer.

Central Massachusetts

Central Massachusetts is more than just an enormous piece of land to drive through on your way from the famous Berkshires towards Boston. This entire region is full of juxtapositions, with bustling metropolitan areas just minutes away from rolling hills, apple orchards, traditional small towns, and rural farmlands. Central Massachusetts is essentially one big transition between the urban lifestyle of Boston and its own city of Worcester and their outlying suburbs and the rural, far western reaches of the state.

Overall, Central Massachusetts can be divided into five areas: Blackstone Valley, Corridor 9, the Johnny Appleseed Trail Region, the Sturbridge Townships, and Worcester. Each area has its own distinct personality and is worth a visit as you explore the state.

The Blackstone Valley is located south of Worcester, in the environs surrounding the Blackstone River. The river, which runs from Worcester to Providence, Rhode Island, is hugely important in terms of American history, as its waters powered the beginning of the American industrial revolution and dramatically transformed this area from an agricultural society to an industrial one in the early nineteenth century.

This entire region is formally called the John H. Chafee Blackstone River Valley National Heritage Corridor (www.nps.gov/blac) and is an official national park, although in a very nontraditional sense. Instead of being actual parklands, protected and only open to the public through the National Park Service, this is a living, breathing national park, where regular citizens live and work and go about their daily lives. The national park area is made up of twenty-four cities and towns in the area surrounding the Blackstone River and is designed to highlight the birthplace of the age of industry for America. It comprises mill towns, dams, trails, and roads, as well as agricultural and natural landscapes. As you explore the area there are plenty of options to choose from, such as historical sites, recreational areas, and museums.

In recent years, this region has been redeveloped to showcase not only its historical significance, but also its recreational side. It's now a great place, with beautiful scenery and impressive wildlife, where you can spend time hiking, canoeing, kayaking, cross-country skiing, and sightseeing.

As you continue to travel north through Central Massachusetts, you'll inevitably end up in the Corridor 9 area, aptly named for its proximity to many bustling highways—I-90, I-495, I-290, and Route 9 for starters. This region is an enormous population center and encompasses the core towns of Westborough, Northborough, Southborough, Shrewsbury, and Grafton. It's primarily known for its geographic accessibility, as it's a great jumping-off point for exploring or working in the rest of the state, but it also has plenty to recommend it on its own, with lots of dining and lodging choices.

You've probably heard of legendary folk hero Johnny Appleseed, the frontier man who spent his life in nature, wandering through Massachusetts (as well as Illinois, Indiana, Kentucky, Ohio, and Pennsylvania) purposefully trailing apple seeds, selling apple trees, and starting orchards wherever he went. Actually named John Chapman, he was born in Leominster, Massachusetts, in the late eighteenth century and left an indelible impression on the character of the state. Even now, centuries later, tourists pack into Massachusetts every spring to view apple blossoms and every autumn to spend an afternoon picking apples at one of the state's many orchards. The Johnny Appleseed Trail runs along Route 2 in the north-central part of the state and passes through many small, traditional New England towns. To learn more about the region, visit the Johnny Appleseed Visitor Center (www.appleseed.org) on the westbound side of Route 2 in Lancaster between exits 35 and 34.

Next up are the Sturbridge Townships. Although Sturbridge itself is essentially just a regular town, the real magic is in Old Sturbridge Village.

- **Old Sturbridge Village** (www.osv.org) is a living-history museum that recreates what it was like to live in an actual 1830s New England village. The village was started in the 1920s by wealthy industrialists looking to preserve a more traditional way of life. They scoured the land to find suitable buildings, collected them on an old farm, and then devoted years to searching for thousands of period antiques to fill the buildings. Their hard work has paid off, and the area is a stunning representation of traditional life in the preindustrial age. But what really makes the area fascinating are the hired actors who populate the village, demonstrating what life was like for the actual settlers. They dress in period costumes, never breaking nineteenth-century character, and demonstrate traditional skills like blacksmithing, weaving, and animal husbandry. This is an all-weather destination, with special holiday demonstrations, winter sleigh rides, and old-time baseball games offered in the summer months.

Within striking distance, and a great place to spend some time or just take an afternoon drive, is the Wachusett Mountain region. The highest peak in southern New England, Wachusett Mountain is a great place to go if you're interested in skiing but don't feel like trekking up to the mountains of the far north.

- **Wachusett Mountain Ski Area** (www.wachusett.com) has twenty-two trails to choose from and could suit both beginner and advanced skiers easily. It's also a great place to head to in the summer, when the slopes are open as hiking trails. From these high points you can take in phenomenal views of Boston to the east and the Berkshires to the west, and all of the rolling countryside in between.

There's also great camping in this part of the state.

- **Wells State Park** (www.mass.gov/dcr/parks/central/well.htm) has sixty campsites scattered throughout the woods and includes a privately owned lake strictly for the use of campers.

And finally, we round up our explorations of Central Massachusetts in Worcester, by far the most well-known area within Central Massachusetts, and with good reason. It's the second largest city in the state, with a sprawling population of more than 170,000 people. Its location is convenient, just one hour from Boston, Providence, and Hartford, and three hours from New York City, makes it a popular location for business meetings and conventions.

Worcester has had a troubled economic history since the end of World War II, and the city still has a gritty, industrial feel. Worcester was never a mill town, unlike many neighboring areas, because it didn't have a strong enough water source to power a mill. Instead it became a manufacturing hub, where all kinds of items were produced, including textiles, carpets, machine tools, boots and shoes, looms, wire products, and ironware. The population swelled with many immigrant laborers, who brought with them their unique trades and ethnic backgrounds, creating a rich diversity that can still be felt in Worcester's many ethnic neighborhoods and restaurants even today. Mix in the youthful energy of the students from the area's eleven colleges and universities, and you end up with an educated and diverse city.

While you're in Worcester and the surrounding areas, you'll have plenty of options for hotels at all ranges of the budget spectrum. All of the big chains can easily be accessed here.

- **Beechwood Hotel** (www.beechwoodhotel.com) is a boutique luxury hotel that offers more personality than the average accomodations. It is also located near all the action in the city of Worcester.

- **The Wachusett Village Inn** (www.wachusettvillageinn.com) is a country inn located in Westminster on one hundred acres of woods near the mountain. It's a perfect place to unwind after spending a day hiking the nearby trails.

- **Sturbridge Country Inn** (www.sturbridgecountryinn.com), in Sturbridge, is ideal if you'd like to try out a local bed-and-breakfast.

- **The Publick House** (www.publickhouse.com) another option in Sturbridge, is an eighteenth-century historic inn with seventeen guest rooms and suites.

There is absolutely no shortage of things to do in Worcester and the surrounding areas.

- **Worcester Art Museum** (www.worcesterart.org) is an amazing, well-respected museum that showcases both contemporary and classic masterpieces.

- **Fruitlands Museum** (www.fruitlands.org) is a complex that was one of the original sites of the Transcendentalist movement, led by Bronson Alcott in the early nineteenth century. Here you'll find a collection of Native American artifacts, a building that houses materials on the Harvard Shakers, and a gallery that includes Hudson River School landscape paintings and the nation's second-largest collection of nineteenth-century folk portraits.

- **DCU Center** (www.dcucenter.com) is a major stop for national music tours and festivals.

- **Higgins Armory Museum** (www.higgins.org) is dedicated to the arms and armor of the medieval and Renaissance periods. You can even sign up for a workshop to learn the art of historical combat in their program called Academy of the Sword, should you be so inclined; or take your kids to CastleKids Story Hour, where for

$12 one adult and one child can enjoy stories of adventure and knighthood along with some crafts and a snack.

- **EcoTarium** (www.ecotarium.org) is the place to go to take in a little wildlife. It is an indoor-outdoor museum in the urban center of Worcester that showcases wildlife and also has a tree canopy walkway, where you can walk high up in the trees on a series of forty-foot-high connected bridges.

- **Broad Meadow Wildlife Sanctuary** (www.massaudubon.org) is located south of Worcester and run by the Massachusetts Audubon Society. The largest urban wildlife sanctuary in New England, you can wander through trails on hundreds of acres of woods, visiting interpretive centers and taking in the nature and wildlife.

- **Miss Worcester Diner** (300 Southbridge Street) is a good place for a quick bite to eat. The diner industry in America essentially began in Worcester in 1906 when the Worcester Lunch Car Company started making lunch wagons. They produced 650 diners before their closing in 1961. This one, made in 1948 and now listed in the National Register of Historic Places, stands across the street from the factory that built it.

John Harvard's Brewery & Ale House

Shoppers World, One Worcester Road,
Framingham, MA 01701
508-875-2337 • www.johnharvards.com

Tucked in the back corner of an outdoor mall filled with large chain stores is the second Massachusetts location of this chain brewpub. To learn the company history please read the Cambridge location entry on page 113.

This location is a fine place to stop in for a quick bite after a day of power shopping. The quick, attentive service is better than the typical commercial pub food being presented from the kitchen. We got a kick out of the stained glass panels featuring "patron saints" like Jerry Garcia, John F. Kennedy, and Theodore J. Roosevelt.

Beers Brewed: John Harvard's Pale Ale, All American Light Lager, Nut Brown Ale, Dry Irish Stout, Old Willy India Pale Ale, Mid-Winter's Strong Ale, Celtic Red, Queen Bee Honey Beer, Wheat Beer, Summer Blonde, Oktoberfest, Holiday Red.

We weren't able to meet with brewer Maria Poulinas when we came through the area, but we had heard great things about her reputation in advance. The beers, which skew towards Belgian styles, were served at the correct temperature, making their flavors and aromas immediately apparent. She's won medals in the past for her beers, and it is clear to see why.

John Harvard's Brewery & Ale House

Opened: 1996.

Owner: Centerplate.

Brewer: Maria Poulinas.

System: 14-barrel pub brewing system.

Production: 900 barrels in 2011.

Hours: Monday through Thursday, 11:30 A.M. to 12:30 A.M.; Friday and Saturday, 11:30 A.M. to 1 A.M.; Sunday, 11:30 A.M. to midnight.

Tours: By appointment.

Take-out beer: Growlers.

Special considerations: Handicapped-accessible.

Parking: Ample free parking, with entrances off Route 9 and Route 30.

Other area beer sites: See the entry for Jack's Abby Brewing Company on page 79.

Nashoba Valley Winery

100 Wattaquadock Hill Road, Bolton, MA 01740
978-779-5521 • www.nashobawinery.com

We arrived at the Nashoba Valley Winery and parked in a field along a row of dwarf apple trees. Exiting the car, we were overwhelmed by the smell of earth. Overhead, thick and fluffy clouds sat lazily in a clear blue sky. Across a small pond was the guesthouse, a sprawling country affair, and on its lawn people lay spread out on blankets or sat at picnic tables. Inside a gazebo, the five-piece band was preparing for their second set. As we walked down a gravel path towards the liquid refreshment, the band kicked off with a pop-ish rendition of Bob Seger's

"C'est La Vie." Soon they were playing tunes from Van Morrison, Old Crow Medicine Show, and Bruce Springsteen, and while it would have been nice to simply grab a bottle and join the crowds on the lawn whiling away the afternoon, we had a brewery to tour and beer to drink.

The brewer here is Thomas Knight, who honed his skills for two years as an "intense" homebrewer before he was hired here. Nashoba's been around since 1978, when it began producing fruit wines, and through the years it's been showered with awards and accolades. In 2000, the owners installed a 15-barrel system purchased at auction from a now-closed brewery in New Hampshire. The two-room brewhouse is inside a cedar shake building that was once the farm's garage. The original farmhouse is now the restaurant.

Beers Brewed: Heron Ale, Bolt 117 Lager, Wattaquadock Wheat, IPA, Belgian Pale Ale, Dunkelweizen, Summer Stout, Oaktoberfest, Imperial Stout.

The Pick: Imperial Stout is thick, boozy, strong, and perfect for after dinner or when it's "just one of those days."

Nashoba has been cranking out an impressive amount of beer on the system, with at least seven different styles on tap when we visited, plus English apple cider. In fact, the fifty-two-acre farm reserves four rows of apples specifically for cider production. They also make perry, or pear cider. It's difficult to come by pear cider in the states. Nashoba's perry is dry, sweet, and tart—refreshing on a warm summer day and versatile enough to be a comfort on a chilly autumn afternoon.

The flagship brews are the Heron Ale, named for a blue heron who hangs out in the winery's ponds, and the Bolt 117 lager, named for the town and its main road. These are perfectly sessionable beers, easy drinking and refreshing on a hot summer's day. But Knight excels at darker beers. His Dunkelweizen was almost chewy with generous amounts of caramel malts. His Imperial Stout pours like a moonless midnight, and with its pleasantly boozy aroma and thick mouthfeel, it should be taken home and cellared to pull out on frozen New England nights.

This farm brewery does as much as possible to keep things local. Spent grain is sent down the road to the Jobarb Farm, and the hogs that receive it as feed return to the restaurant as pork. In addition to the one hundred different varieties of apples, grapes, pears and other produce grown at the farm, Knight also harvests his own supply of hops. You'll see trellises near the main entrance and others scattered throughout the property. At the time of our visit, he had two hundred hops plants growing, yielding Centennial, Nugget, Chinook, Newport, and Fuggle varieties.

Around harvest season, Knight makes wet hop beers, meaning they are done with fresh hops not dried ones, which yields rich, floral flavors with aromas of fresh vegetation.

The brewery has a limited distribution. The beers are on tap in some locations, and bottles are available at others, but to get the full range, you must head to the winery itself.

J's Restaurant is on the property, giving patrons an opportunity to pair the offerings with well-prepared dishes. Picnic lunches are offered during warm weather. Customers are allowed to bring their own food as well.

During a day at the winery, we saw people enjoying the grounds, strolling the fields, or just settling in with cheese and crackers and other snacks to accompany the bottles purchased inside the gift store. It was heartening to see that there was a 60/40 split in the number of wine drinkers versus beer drinkers. It shows not only the willingness of people to try new beers but also that Knight's talent as a brewer brings people back for more.

Inside the brewery, we couldn't help but notice the two racks of barrels resting along a wall. Knight explained that new barrels come in and are used first for white wines. After a few uses, they go to the red wines. Then, they are moved over to the distillery.

Beer, wine, and spirits? Nashoba is a triple threat! If you're able, try the single malt whisky, aged five years when we tasted it. Let its smoky aroma surround you like a comfortable blanket.

After the distillery, which Knight also mans, the brewery gets the barrels to age beers. Knight had some ideas on what would be filling the most recent ones, but he held those cards close to the vest. And that's incentive enough to come back.

Nashoba Valley Winery

Opened: 2002.

Owner: Richard Pelletier.

Brewer: Thomas Knight.

System: 15-barrel New World Brewing System, tanks by JV Northwest and Canada Criveller Company, and 1996 Meheen Manufacturing bottling line.

Production: 300 barrels in 2011.

Hours: Open every day from 10 A.M. to 5 P.M.

Tours: Two tours given in the summer each year, led by the brewer. See the website for dates and additional information.

Take-out beer: Growlers and bottles.

Extras: Annual Oktoberfest with beer garden and live music.

Special considerations: Handicapped-accessible.

Parking: On site.

Other area beer sites:

- **River Rock Grill** (163 Main Street Maynard, 978-897-5500, www.theriver rockgrill.com) is open for lunch and dinner and serves Nashoba and other craft beers on draught. When the weather is right, sit on the deck while you eat and drink and enjoy the gentle sounds of the nearby Assabet River.

Wormtown Brewery

455 Park Avenue, Worcester, MA 01610
774-239-1555 • www.wormtownbrewery.com

If all goes according to plan, Wormtown Brewery will be the last job Ben Roesch puts on his résumé. That's not to say he wouldn't have an impressive résumé without it, but after a decade in the industry and working for several other Massachusetts breweries, he finally has a brewery of his own and going back to working for someone else just isn't in the cards.

Roesch started out working at a homebrew spot around 2000 and eventually landed an assistant brewer job at the Cambridge Brewing Company. From there he was off to Wachusett, and after that he took the head brewing and distilling position at the Nashoba Valley Winery. After a few years there, he left to consult with a brewery in Southbridge and then became brewer at the now-defunct Honest Town. "I definitely cut my teeth trying to get to the next level professionally," Roesch said.

Now he's at his own place, a 2,500-barrel-per-year brewery in what used to be an ice cream parlor connected to Peppercorns Bar and Grill. It is also, remarkably, the first brewery in modern memory to open in Worcester. For a college town with a good infrastructure, industry, and a strong residential base, it seems like a place where a

Beers Brewed: Seven Hills Pale Ale, Be Hoppy IPA, Turtle Boy Blueberry Ale, Worcester's Bravest Ale, Elm Park Amber Ale, Wormtown Pumpkin Ale, Wintah Ale, O'Connor's Irish Red Ale, Blonde Cougar Summer Ale, Woosta Weizenbock, Be Hoppier IPA, O'fest, Local First, The Buk, Red Headed Bitch, Dark Day Black IPA, Beer Goggles Barleywine, Foxy Brown Imperial Maple Ale, Mass Whole.

brewery would have opened a long time ago. In naming his brewery, Roesch harkened back to the 1970s, calling the venture Wormtown, a nickname for Worcester born during the punk movement and given by a local deejay.

The Pick: It's the ten gallons of maple syrup (from Ewens Sleepy Hollow Maple Farm in Lancaster) that makes the Foxy Brown Maple Ale the boozy, sweet, warm, and deep beer that it is. Go slow and enjoy every sip!

"I could have gone the route and called it Worcester Brewing or something," he said. "But Wormtown felt like Worcester, it fit, it felt unique." That said, his beers, like Seven Hills Pale Ale or Elm Park Amber Ale, carry names that have something to do with the city. "Our main focus is Worcester," Roesch said.

The city has responded in kind. He's on tap in dozens of places around the city and slowly expanding beyond its limits, but Roesch said that he would always favor his city when it comes to making sure people have a fresh supply.

Although it is hard to miss Wormtown beers around the city, you need only be a few steps from the fermentation tanks themselves at the adjacent Peppercorn's Grille and Tavern (455 Park Avenue, 508-752-7711, www.epeppercorns.com) to get the full gamut of Wormtown beers. Peppercorn's has a modern, stylish look with a granite bar. Sitting there, your back is to a window into the brewery, partially obscured by kegs. It feels like a place for locals, but strangers are just as welcome. Keno is broadcast on televisions in the bar area.

Roesch makes sure that Peppercorn's has every beer he brews on tap and this includes some rare offerings or limited releases, such as the Foxy Brown Maple Ale and Mass Whole Ale, brewed with ingredients completely harvested in the commonwealth. Peppercorns also has a great craft bottle selection, but with all this fresh beer, stick with the taps. Soon Roesch will be offering 22-ounce bottles and hopes the brewery grows enough to warrant a true industrial space. He'll stay in the Worcester area, of course.

"We want to be here for the long run," he explained. "We don't want to see our personal bubble burst. The beer's quality should stand the test of time and we wanted to be known for making something good and not cutting corners, staying true to who are."

Wormtown Brewery

Opened: 2010.
Owners: Ben Roesch and Tom Oliveri.
Brewers: Ben Roesch, Ben Pratt, and Damase Olsson.

System: Custom designed by Ben Roesch, with dual direct-fire gas burner kettle, electric hot liquor tank, single-step infusion mash tun, and converted Grundy extra electric hot liquor tank (for brewing twice a day).

Production: 1,400 barrels in 2011.

Hours: You can sample all of Wormtown's beers at the adjacent Peppercorn's Grille & Tavern. Peppercorn's is open Monday through Thursday, 11:30 A.M. to 11 P.M. and Friday through Sunday, noon to 11 P.M.

Tours: By appointment.

Take-out beer: Growlers.

Special considerations: Handicapped-accessible.

Parking: Plenty on site.

Other area beer sites:

- **The Armsby Abbey** (144 North Main Street, Worcester, 508-795-1012, www. armsbyabbey.com).
- **The BlackStone Tap** (81 Water Street, Worcester, 508-797-4827, www.black stonetap.com).
- **Brew City Grill & Brew House** (104 Shrewsbury Street, Worcester, 508-752-3862, www.brew-city.com).
- **The Dive Bar** (34 Green Street, Worcester, thedivebarworcester.com).
- **O'Connor's Restaurant and Bar** (1160 West Boylston Street, Worcester, 508-853-0789, www.oconnorsrestaurant.com).

Wachusett Brewing Company

175 State Road East, Westminster, MA 01473
978-874-9965 • www.wachusettbrew.com

This is what you get when three engineering students get together and decide to take their fondness for beer and combine it with industrial know-how. Wachusett Brewing Company is best known in the state and region for its blueberry ale, but it is so much more than that.

As we pulled up to the brewery, we took it as a good sign that a cyclist in a Harpoon Brewery jersey zoomed past. Clearly this area knows good beer. But, we were admittedly confused by the building, a three-story redbrick and glass structure with a modern look, which seemed more suited for law offices or a medical practice.

True to that form, we sat in the brewery tasting room, which served as a waiting room, surrounded by well-polished furniture, with news clippings from over the years framed on the walls and music piping in from nearby speakers. After a few minutes we were met by Dave Higgins, the brewer, who gave us a few samples poured from the adjoining tasting room before bringing us back into the brewing area.

As we passed through the wide doors, the corporate structure yielded to a rough-around-the-edges brewery—just the way we like it. Within a minute we saw the proof that engineers make smart brewers. This includes the use of a shrimp steamer, now turned on its side, in the brewing process. There are pulleys, levers, and platforms that create a mosaic of metal, piping, and electrical work. An old soda filler has been retrofitted as a bottle machine and after some tinkering and retinkering can now fill five hundred bottles a minute.

Ned LaFortune, Kevin Buckler, and Peter Quinn founded Wachusett Brewing Company in 1994, having been inspired by other breweries. In the beginning the trio worked tirelessly to build the brand, self-distributed the beers in growlers, and managed to grow the business through the support of volunteers to build a brewery that today employs a few dozen workers and produces beer available throughout the Northeast. Each owner brings his own strengths to the brewery and takes a different approach to growing it from beyond where it is today. Peter is the sales manager; Ned is the planner, thinking about the brewery ten years from now; and Kevin is the "here and now" guy.

Wachusett has built a following by being consistent and not releasing too many odd offerings. By not taking a page from some West Coast breweries that are constantly rolling out brews with different ingredients or hybrid styles, they have been able to concentrate on their core brands—reliable recipes in reliable styles.

"We're fairly fuddy-duddy-like," Higgins told us. "We create beers that you can have more than one of and enjoy yourself. It's about the flavor for us."

Beers Brewed: Blueberry, Country Pale Ale, IPA, Green Monsta IPA, Ryde Beer, Black Shack Porter, Nut Brown Ale, Summer Ale, Octoberfest, Winter Ale, Quinn's Amber Ale, Milk Stout, Larry Imperial IPA, Imperial Pumpkin.

The Pick: Ryde Beer is crisp, clean, dry, and can be enjoyed anytime, but feels particularly satisfying after a long stretch on a bike.

Wachusett Brewing Company

Opened: 1994.

Owners: Ned LaFortune, Kevin Buckler, and Peter Quinn.

Brewers: Master Brewer, Dave Howard; brewers, Dave Higgins, Pete Mattison, and Ron Gamble.

System: Custom system

Production: 23,000 barrels in 2011.

Hours: Wednesday and Saturday, noon to 5 P.M.; Thursday and Friday, noon to 6 P.M.

Tours: Wednesday through Saturday, noon to 4 P.M.

Take-out beer: Bottles, growlers and kegs.

Extras: Tasting room is available for hosting private parties, gatherings, or corporate events.

Special considerations: Handicapped-accessible.

Parking: Plenty on site.

Other area beer sites:

- **The 1761 Old Mill** (69 State Road East, Westminster, 978-874-5941, www.1761 oldmill.com) is a scenic site down the street from the brewery and a good place to have a bite and drink a pint.

Pioneer Brewing Company

195 Arnold Road, Fiskdale, MA 01518
508-347-7500 • www.pioneerbrewingcompany.com

The groups arrived tired and sweaty, but mostly happy after a rousing round of disc golf. The emerging sport, a sort of fusion between Frisbee and golf, is gaining traction nationwide. There is a course here in Central Massachusetts, and it so happens that it's conveniently located adjacent to Pioneer Brewing, giving players a chance to relive victories or console a loss.

The brewery's tasting room is a great place to spend a few hours. Wood-paneled walls adorned with historical beer trays—everything from Schaefer to Sam Adams—along the ceiling give it kind of a 1950s basement hangout feeling. Kitschy touches like a Schlitz clock and some stained glass signs add to the grandfather's rec room atmosphere.

Pioneer was previously known as Hyland's Brewery. It got its start in 1996 under the Damon family, who has since 1945 owned the orchard, land, farm, and park where the brewery sits today. In 2004, the family decided to focus their attention elsewhere, but rather than close the

Beers Brewed: Pale Ale, Red Ale, Kolsch, India Pale Ale, Nitro Stout, Blueberry Ale, Dark Harvest, Doppelbock, Belgian Wit, Oktoberfest, Hop Whammy.

brewery, they let brewer Todd Sullivan and his friend Tim Daley take over operations. It was renamed Pioneer around that time, and it has retained a loyal following and a reputation as a solid contract brewery.

One other plus about Pioneer is their mug club. It's a staple of most brewpubs and quite a few breweries, where regulars are rewarded for frequent patronage. Often these come with a regular drink discount. Other benefits can include invitations to tappings, special beer dinners, meal discounts, or free logo merchandise. Plus, there is the general feeling of superiority, a way of saying, "I come here a lot. They know my name."

Mug clubs are a great way to get more from a brewery experience. Often the gatherings hosted for members turn into jolly conversations about homebrewing, beer travel, and unique brews found in local stores, and over time, strangers become friends. The nominal fee that most places charge pays for itself after only a few visits.

We had an enjoyable afternoon learning about disc golf (there are nearly twenty courses in the state) while quaffing beers like the 5 percent Belgian Wit. "Good beer, good people, and disc golf. What could be any better?" asked Brad Parsons, a Pioneer regular, before heading out to the course.

Pioneer Brewing Company

Opened: 1996.

Owners: Todd Sullivan and Tim Daley.

Brewer: Todd Sullivan and Tim Daley.

Hours: Tuesday through Friday, 3 P.M. to 9 P.M.; Saturday, noon to 9 P.M.; Sunday, noon to 8 P.M. Closed Mondays.

Tours: Offered by appointment for groups of twelve or more.

Special considerations: Handicapped-accessible.

Parking: On-site lot.

Gardner Ale House Brewery and Restaurant

74 Parker Street, Gardner, MA 01440
978-669-0122 • www.gardnerale.com

At night they move the tables and chairs away from their usual spots in front of the brewing equipment and let the bands set up. Yes, in this day and age where restaurant space is at a premium and most places would rather have butts in seats with a constant flow of food and drink coming their way, the Gardner Ale House keeps the music alive. That, in turn, brings in the crowds, which helps, not hurts, the bottom line, despite the loss of a few tables.

One thing that took us by surprise about this brewpub in the blue-collar town of Gardner was its age. It opened in 2006, and despite its youth, it feels like it has been around at least four times that long. It's not to say that the place feels rundown, because it doesn't. It feels comfortable, lived in, and loved. It's a place where people come to relax and unwind over near-perfect pints made by brewmaster and co-owner Dave Richardson.

This quintessential neighborhood spot doesn't discriminate either. When we visited for the first time, the bartender treated us like we had been coming in since the opening. He expertly walked us through the beer list and made a few great food suggestions. The hummus sandwich and the braumeister, with slow-roasted prime rib and smoked Gouda, were outstanding. A variety of specialty pizzas are available as well, and are not to be missed.

The building is split into three distinct parts, and was likely once three different stores, but the brewery has been using all three sections "for as long as anyone alive can remember," said Richardson. Walking through the main entrance, you're met with the wide and generous wood bar, shaped like a backwards J. The brewing equipment serves as the backdrop for live music.

To the left is the dining area and beyond that is the visible kitchen. The owners have kept much of

Beers Brewed: Facelift IPA, Oma's Altbier, Face-off Double IPA, Oktoberfest, Nightcrawler, Chocolate Porter, Chair City Pale Ale, The Belgian Chair, The Hef, Old School Pilsner, Dave's Double, Summer's End Kolsch.

The Pick: Kolsch is considered one of the hardest styles to master and consistently brew, but at Gardner, Summer's End is a beer of clear beauty, crisp and refreshing. If it's on tap, it should be in your glass.

the original building details, which give the place a great historic feel. Walls of exposed brick and wooden beams, the old-growth, wide-plank wood floor, and period wainscoting all add to the charm of the brewpub.

We caught up with Richardson after our first visit, when we'd already had a chance to try some of his beers. The first thing he wanted to point out is that he doesn't filter the beers. So, some will be clear if they have had ample time to rest, but others will be cloudy. He finds himself explaining it to first-time customers this way: "It's the difference between apple juice and apple cider."

Lest you think you'll find any sour or off-flavors in his beer, we'll set the record straight and say that you won't. Richardson, like so many other brewers of his generation, got started the right way as a homebrewer. He was actually brought into it by friend and Ale House co-owner Rick Walton. The two would brew together and drink and talk about the pipe dream of having their own place. Finally fed up with his job as a lab worker, Richardson quit, took out a loan, and got his masters in brewing from the University of California–Davis. He moved back east and spent three years brewing for Red Hook in New Hampshire. Then, Walton called and said a restaurant space had opened in Gardner that would be perfect for a brewery, and soon Richardson found himself running his own equipment.

It's been a marathon since they opened. It takes long days and nights to make sure that things run smoothly, the food is just right, and the beers are true to style. There is pride behind Richardson's tired voice.

"It is how a pub is supposed to be, used to be," he said. "There was a little pub in every town where people hung out when they weren't working. Our place is not about going and getting drunk. It is about having a few good beers while socializing."

Gardner Ale House Brewery and Restaurant

Opened: 2006.

Owners: Rick Walton and Dave Richardson.

Brewer: Dave Richardson.

System: 7-barrel Pub System.

Production: 560 barrels in 2011.

Hours: Sunday through Thursday, 11:30 A.M. to 11 P.M.; Friday and Saturday, 11:30 A.M. to midnight.

Tours: By appointment only.

Take-out beer: Half-gallon growlers of anything on tap less than 8 percent alcohol. No growler sales on Sunday.

Extras: Live music.

Special considerations: Handicapped-accessible.

Parking: Free across the street in the municipal lot.

Jack's Abby Brewing

81 Morton Street, Framingham, MA 01702
508-872-0900 • www.jacksabbybrewing.com

Three brothers helm this relatively new brewery, but it's actually named after one of their wives. That would be Abby, Jack Hendler's wife. The brewery name is also a nod to the monastic brewing tradition, but lest you think it revolves around the more familiar Belgian tradition, Jack set the record straight. "People seem to forget the tradition of German monastic brewing," he said, standing in the brewery tasting room near a few brewery posters illustrating his point. He talked about how these breweries were responsible for introducing lagers to the world, promoting the use of hops, and standardizing brewing procedures.

Jack believes that American brewers have largely forgotten the contributions of old German breweries, so he wanted to pay homage to them and follow their styles. Lederhosen hanging on a peg next to the brewery entrance is another nod to these forefathers.

Jack is the brewer, brother Sam concentrates on sales, and brother Eric spreads the good word of the brewery. The family is not new to the beverage industry. Their grandfather, father, and uncle helmed the New York–based Saxony Ice Company for decades, and they honed their business and work ethic by starting at the bottom and doing the jobs that needed to be done. The family would eventually sell the business but kept the entrepreneurial spirit.

Jack was bit by the brewing bug in college and began homebrewing. He and Abby traveled the world, visiting breweries for a decade, learning the

Beers Brewed: Jabby Brau, Hoponius Union, Smoke & Dagger, Framinghammer Baltic Porter, Hey Diddle Diddle, Red Tape Lager, Copper Legend, Saxon Sons Pilsner, Wet Hop Lager.

The Pick: The beechwood-smoked malt makes all the difference in the Smoke & Dagger, a black lager that is hearty and smoky and goes perfect with barbeque.

process and watching masters at work. Photos from those journeys can be seen hanging on the wall of the tasting room. Jack eventually went to brewing school to learn the technical skills necessary to brew on a large scale. At the time, Sam was studying community development and applied economics at the University of Vermont and Eric was working for a small financial firm. By early 2011, the brothers were ready to open the brewery.

Jack's Abby is an impressively large 4,500-square-foot space that still felt cavernous after they installed a 20-barrel brewhouse and five 40-barrel fermentation tanks. It's "go big or go home" with these brothers. Right now they are focusing on draft accounts in the metro west area and also provide growler fills from the brewery. With all the extra space, it's a good bet a bottling line will be added in the near future. One personal touch that stood out early on was a mural painted on the wall opposite the fermentation tanks. Done by a local artist, the brothers said the "canvas" would be painted over from time to time, allowing different artists to showcase their talents.

Jack clearly prefers German-style beers, and his first lineup is very lager heavy. It's a refreshing change from many breweries that focus on ales. With one eye on tradition, the other is on American brewing innovation. He offers a pilsner, an India pale lager, a smoked black lager, and a 100-percent dark Munich malt-brewed lager with glacier hops that gives off a sweet floral aroma. The inaugural brew was the Red Tape Lager, a 5 percent ABV nod to the local government hurdles that were conquered in advance of opening.

We can expect good things hopswise from this brewery, as the family owns a farm in southwestern Vermont that's home to a thriving crop. After a visit to Washington State in 2005, Jack brought back a cascade hop rhizome with him. He planted it on the farm, where it took root and flourished. These days the farm has eight rows of sixteen-foot-high trellises stretching 130 feet with twenty-five vines each on the half-acre parcel of land. Currently they're growing Centennial, Cascade, and Willamette varieties. Jack told us he plans to do as much as he can with these family hops, so future pints should have a truly fresh hop flavor.

There will likely be other fresh flavors in the beers as well. Just outside of the brewery, inside a fenced-in spit of land, is the family garden, where they're growing rosemary, parsley, sage, thyme, and even oats. The brothers smiled as they passed each plant, eagerly talking about what ingredient would go in which beer.

Despite entering a crowded and established beer market, Jack's Abby has the determination, inventiveness, and passion to make a real impact and impression on local palates.

Jack's Abby Brewing

Opened: 2011.

Owners: Jack, Eric, and Sam Hendler.

Brewers: Jack Hendler.

System: Premier Stainless.

Production: 500 barrels in 2011.

Hours: Thursday and Friday, 3 P.M. to 7 P.M.; Saturday, noon to 5 P.M.

Tours: Thursday and Friday, 3 P.M. to 7 P.M.; Saturday, noon to 5 P.M.

Take-out beer: Growlers and bottles.

Extras: Tasting room.

Special considerations: Handicapped-accessible.

Parking: On site.

Other area beer sites:
- **British Beer Company** (120 Worcester Road, Framingham, 508-879-1776, britishbeer.com).
- **O'Connell's Pub** (700 Worcester Road, Framingham, 508-283-1079, www.oconnellspubonline.com).
- **The Chicken Bone** (358 Waverly Street, Framingham, 1-800-WINGS-2-U, www.thechickenbone.com).
- **The Tavern** (102 Irving Street, Framingham, 774-999-0705, www.thetavern framingham.net).

Brew-on-Premises Establishments

Brew-on-premises establishments occupy an interesting middle ground bet-ween homebrewing and full-fledged craft breweries. They are establish-ments where the equipment and ingredients are already stocked and waiting for would-be brewers to use. These operations include eager staff willing to help out with the finer points or act as full-on instruc-tors. Massachusetts has two such locations, and they are great spots for beginners to learn the trade or groups of friends to gather and do something different.

Above all else, it is the chance to make something and call it your own. You later bottle the beer you brew and bring it home. Then you can share with friends and family and take credit when they exclaim, "Hey, this isn't half bad!"

- **Barleycorn's Craft Brew** (21 Summer Street, Natick, MA 01760; 508-651-8885; www.barleycorn.com). Dan Eng had experience running a bar and restau-rant but the brewing concept was somewhat distant to him when he arrived in California back in 1997 for a 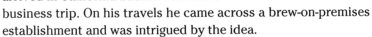 business trip. On his travels he came across a brew-on-premises establishment and was intrigued by the idea.

  Basically, customers would come in and work with a brewer to create a beer, doing everything from measuring ingredients to hop additions and watching the boil. It was a simple concept and a popular one. Eng knew it would work in Massachusetts. The next year he opened Barleycorn's Craft Brew, bringing some of the West Coast back to the East.

  With his six brew kettles, he can accommodate several groups at once. After people pick their recipe and brew (Barleycorn's uses a partial mash, so the process only takes about two hours), they come back a few weeks later to help bottle and then can take home their wares to share with family and friends.

"Their eyes light up," Eng said of customers who taste their beer for the first time. "They are really happy and impressed with how good it is."

Barleycorn's gets a lot of first-timers who are interested in brewing. Some get bitten by the homebrewing bug and even go on to making a career of it. Others become casual visitors, coming back every few months to brew a new batch.

Eng said it is easy to see where the overall beer scene is headed. When he started there was a focus on pale ales, brown ales, and beers that were readily available in the marketplace. Today it's about "extreme beers," high-alcohol doozies that either have a personal spin or are copies of beers made in other states.

Getting together with friends for a brew day is a perfect way to spend a few hours, and a place like Barleycorn's is the perfect place to do it.

- **Deja Brew** (510 B Boston Turn-
pike Road, Shrewsbury, MA 01545;
508-842-8991; www.deja-brew.com).
Ray Schavone found his inspira-
tion in Canada. While on a business trip in the mid-1990s, he walked past a brew-on-premises shop and, already an avid home-brewer, he was intrigued. Upon entering he found a wonderful scene: people sitting around, laughing, talking, drinking, making beer, and enjoying an overall feel of camaraderie. A short time later when he was downsized out of a job, he recalled that Canadian visit and sought to bring the concept to Central Massachusetts.

After learning the ropes about business plans, small business loans, local zoning issues, and construction, he opened Deja Brew in 1997. It has much the same feel, he said, as the Canadian location. At the various brew stations, people do their partial mash brews, while being able to talk with other groups, hang out with friends, enjoy beers left behind by other customers, and have slices of pizza from a shop two doors down. "We're really good for their business," said Schavone.

As for styles, if it exists, you can likely make it at Deja Brew. Customers can pick from more than two hundred different beer recipes; anything from milk stouts to a clone of Stone Brewing Company's Arrogant Bastard is available. "The only thing we don't do is lambics, or a goze," said Schavone.

The staff works with customers to decide on which beer to make. Since they will have to drink it when they get home, it's best, Schavone said, to stay inside a comfort area.

Like other brew-on-premises, Deja Brew gives customers a few hours to work with a brewer and get their beer done. They return after a few weeks to bottle the beer and leave with six cases of their own creation. That is, so long as they are happy with it. "The first question we ask is 'what do you have in your fridge at home?'" Schavone said.

Deja Brew has a policy that states if a customer is not happy with the beer they made when they come to bottle, they can either get a refund or brew another beer. In all his years of operation, Schavone said, he can count on one hand the number of times customers have invoked this privilege.

The clientele is a healthy mix of "newbies," established homebrewers, and the somewhat regular customers. Schavone said there is one group that comes in every six weeks, books up the entire store, and to date has brewed more than five hundred batches.

They also have homebrewers who come in with their own recipes, but want to brew on a larger system. Schavone is happy to accommodate them. Deja Brew also has the ability to make wine on the premises.

With its comfortable interior that includes beer signs on the wall and empty bottles lining shelves, Deja Brew is a cool place to spend an afternoon. Schavone said his motto should be "leave your worries at the door," because everything is taken care of, and it's hard not to have a good time while brewing with friends.

The Greater Merrimack Valley

Head north and west from Boston and in a snappy twenty-five miles (the level of snappiness being traffic-dependent), you'll hit the Merrimack Valley, which runs along the Merrimack River and the Massachusetts–New Hampshire border. Although not large geographically, this part of the state packs an enormous punch in terms of natural beauty and an almost impossible amount of historic attractions.

It's a wonderful thing to leave the urban setting of Boston and, within just a few short miles on a commuter rail or bustling highway, enter a place as deeply historic and New England-style quaint as the Merrimack Valley. While the region is made up of a wealth of towns and cities, nearly all of which have some interesting claim to fame or another, the regional heavy-hitters are Lexington, Concord, and Lowell.

Lexington and Concord, twin cities with distinct and impressive backgrounds, are so stunningly historic that as you walk down their perfectly preserved streets, gazing over real stonewalls into the windows of actual eighteenth-century colonial houses, you feel the curtain between the past and present slide open for awhile. It's easy to imagine yourself in George Washington's time, with Revolutionary War soldiers galloping by on horseback towards the local tavern for a pint. That actually could happen if you are in Lexington, the "Birthplace of American Liberty," on Patriot's Day, April 19. Reenactments of the Battle of Lexington, where the "shot heard 'round the world" rang out, are held regularly, with minutemen fighting the redcoats on the Lexington Green.

Nearby Concord was where the minutemen hid their stash of weapons and ammunition, and it was here that Paul Revere was headed after Lexington, riding his horse to warn the locals about the arrival of the British. Although he was arrested before reaching Concord, it was in part because of his early warning that the minutemen were able to organize quickly and beat the redcoats when they arrived. These two battles marked the beginning of the Revolutionary War, the first time Americans banded together to stand up to the British.

Concord is not only remembered for its part in the Revolutionary War, but in later years for being a major epicenter of literary and philosophical thought. This was home to the likes of Ralph Waldo Emerson, Henry David Thoreau, Nathaniel Hawthorne, and Louisa May Alcott to name just a few.

Currently, these suburban areas are home to many of Boston's wealthy elite. But the entire region is literally overrun with accommodation options, the majority of which actually are restored colonial homes, so you can easily get a sense of that history while you're in town.

Another major player in the Merrimack Valley is city of Lowell, but for completely different reasons. Night and day from the historic colonial vibe of the other cities, Lowell's background and current energy are utterly industrial and urban. This is where the American industrial revolution peaked, and you can easily see evidence of that storied past in factory after factory lining the banks of the Merrimack River and the city's abundant canal system. You can spend hours here (and we did) walking along the canals, viewing the old mills where women worked on textiles that created a boom of wealth for this region in the nineteenth century. The city fell on hard times in the 1920s and only began a revitalization process in the 1990s, now slowly but surely becoming more and more appealing. It's still distinctly urban and almost totally ungentrified. There are opportunities to take in a museum or two, stop in at a gallery, eat at one of its many ethnic restaurants, or just take a stroll along the banks of the canal under the towering mills.

Although Lexington, Concord, and Lowell present a near-perfect picture of the richness of the Merrimack Valley region, there are many other towns worth a mention. It's easy to spend an afternoon driving on the country roads of Acton or Dunstable, walking the apple orchards of Tyngsborough or Stow, strolling the preserved downtown of Maynard and viewing the Old Mill clock tower, or visiting the conservation lands of Groton for an afternoon of hiking, horseback riding, fishing, or swimming. The Merrimack Valley is quintessential New England in a nutshell, and it's a wonderful place to spend some time. Here are some ideas for lodging.

- **Amerscot House Inn** (www.amerscot.com) was where we stayed in the town of Stow, first settled in 1660 and one of the oldest towns in the state. Built in 1734, this bed-and-breakfast is utter perfection for anyone who wants to stay in a restored colonial home but doesn't want the fussiness of a traditional bed-and-breakfast. Simple, classic, and beautiful, this home is in a residential neighborhood and within short driving distance to the major sites in the region. Enjoy your home-cooked breakfast with others at the large plank-style dining table or in private on the screened-in porch overlooking the sprawling yard and woods. Innkeepers Viki and Andy Carter are excellent hosts, giving this friendly establishment an air of professionalism blended with just the right amount of hominess. Although on the pricey side, it's worth every penny to stay here.

- **Concord's Colonial Inn** (www.concordscolonialinn.com), in Concord, is great for some old-fashioned Americana. The hotel, literally draped in American flags of all shapes and sizes, is on the list of Historic Hotels of America, a distinction granted by the National Trust for Historic Preservation.

- **UMass–Lowell Inn & Conference Center** (http://acc-umlinnand conferencecenter.com), in Lowell, is clean, huge, and modern. It is conveniently located near all of the major sites and has great amenities.

Here are some attractions in the Merrimack Valley you may want to consider exploring between your brewery visits.

- **Lowell National Historical Park** (www.nps.gov/lowe) explains the historical significance of the city and its industrial heritage. The visitor center is located downtown, and the park itself is composed of old mill buildings, as well as other cultural sights and historic scenes. Take a guided tour or just pick up a map and wander along, as we did, to get a sense of the city.

- **Jack Kerouac Commemorative**, in Lowell, is a series of stone monoliths along the waterfront engraved with passages from his writings. Lowell is where the legendary author of *On the Road* and other books that defined the Beat Generation grew up. Much of his later fiction was set here. In his later years, Kerouac returned to Lowell and died here.

- **Lowell Folk Festival** (www.lowellfolkfestival.org) in July is a combination of music, ethnic foods, and art exhibits that is the largest festival of its kind in the country—and a great celebration of the multiculturalism of Lowell itself.

- **Lexington Historical Society** (www.lexingtonhistory.org) offers a tour of the town's historic houses, taverns, and other buildings from the days of the American Revolution.

- **Lexington Battle Green** (www.libertyride.us/historic.html) is a park in the city center where an American flag flies twenty-four hours a day by order of Congress, with monuments honoring that first important battle.

- **Minuteman National Historical Park** (www.nps.gov/mima) in Concord commemorates the battle of that fateful April day in 1775 when the fighting began. The infrastructure of the park is the same as it was all those years ago, so you can easily imagine the scenes of battle while strolling through this area.

- **Walden Pond State Reservation** (www.mass.gov), in Concord, is the site of Thoreau's cabin (no longer standing) and the pond made famous by his book *Walden*.

- **Orchard House** (www.louisamayalcott.org), in Concord, is where Louisa May Alcott wrote her classic *Little Women*.

- **Sleepy Hollow Cemetery** in Concord is the place to visit the graves of all four famous authors, buried together in a section called Author's Ridge. Or just wander the town, which is an atmospheric blend of bookshops and cafes along winding streets, and just soak up the literary greatness.

Ipswich Ale Brewery

23 Hayward Street, Ipswich, MA 01938
(978) 356-3329, www.mercurybrewing.com

One needs a map to navigate the business that is Ipswich Ales. Not only do they produce the namesake line of ales, but also a label called Stone Cat. They produce Mercury Soda Pop and Ipswich Ale Stone Ground Mustard, and they contract for nearly a dozen other breweries under the Mercury Brewing Company label.

Clearly we would need a guide, so naturally we turned to Rob Martin, the brewery president, to help us find fermented enlightenment.

"We're coming out with a new line as well, called 5 Mile, and the premise behind it is that ingredients are Massachusetts grown and at least one will come from within five miles of the brewery," said Martin. So for those keeping score early on, that's three different brands of house beer. Ipswich, said Martin, is more of the traditional brand. This lineup includes IPA, Oatmeal Stout, other offerings for each season, and one simply called Original, which is an unfiltered English pale ale that has great malt characteristics and a little hoppiness.

Next up is the Stone Cat line of beers, which Martin describes as "oddball and different," such as Blueberry Ale, Hefeweizen, Scotch Ale, and Octoberfest, to name just a few.

Martin said each label appeals to different customers so they are not actually fighting themselves for shelf space. The 5 Mile will appeal to the locavore movement, which Martin said "is coming at us like a freight train." With the emerging desire for locally sourced food, Martin said, this will be important in keeping down energy costs and prices while supporting local economies and giving customers the direct knowledge of where the ingredients come from.

Mercury takes a similar approach with their sodas. Made locally in flavors like black cherry, lemon lime, raspberry, and birch beer, their pop is a sweet treat. "Overall we're in the business of making beverages," said Martin.

To that end, they have also carved themselves a niche in the local contract-brewing market. Under the Mercury Brewing Company banner they are brewing, fermenting, and bottling beer for nearly a dozen different breweries that lack a brick-and-mortar facility of their own. Familiar Ipswich-based names like Clown Shoes and Notch are made inside Mercury's walls.

Some brewers are hands on, coming in with recipes, spending brew days among the tanks, and shoveling mash. Others come with a concept and let Mercury's staff brewers devise or refine styles and do all the work. Still others are in the middle of those two worlds. Martin said his brewery is flexible and glad to help these brewers get their beer to market. "The world needs good beer," he said. "If there is someone who wants us to brew good beer we're all for it."

Beers Brewed: Ipswich: Original Ale, IPA, Dark Ale, Oatmeal Stout, Summer Ale, Harvest Ale, Winter Ale. Stone Cat: Blonde Ale, Blueberry Ale, I.P.A., E.S.B., Octoberfest, Hefeweizen, Pumpkin Ale, Scotch Ale, Winter Lager. 5 Mile: Stock Ale.

The Pick: The Harvest Ale is the best of both worlds. Using a darker Caramunich malt and just a touch of chocolate malt in the recipe, they add a blend of Warrior, Ahtanum, and Columbus hops. The result is a happy marriage of malt and hops that can please even the most discerning of palates.

The world also needs good mustard and on that front Ipswich has you covered as well. Around the year 2000 they released a stone-ground mustard. Seeds are soaked in oatmeal stout and then brought to a stone-grinding facility in Maine, where they are turned into the spicy sandwich topper. Lest you dismiss this as just another condiment, it is worth noting that it took top honors at the Napa Valley World-Wide Mustard Competition, beating out nearly five hundred other competitors.

But why mustard? "We're always trying different vehicles to get our name out there," Martin said, leading us into a perfect segue.

Ipswich has a fleet of historic four-wheeled trucks and vans, with classic paint jobs and built-in taps that serve not only festivals and beer events, but are also available for weddings and private parties. The original tapmobile, a 1965 Grumman Kurbside truck, is called "Thing." In a previous life, it was used as a tool truck, and when the brewery was founded in 1991, it became the first delivery truck. It spent the next eleven years carting around bottles and kegs. When it finally kicked out for the last time, it sat unmovable next to the building. One autumn, with winter approaching, Martin said he looked at the old Grumman and realized that he'd have to plow around it after each snowstorm. "I could fix it or get rid of it," he said, "and I couldn't get rid of it." So just about everything was replaced and the Grumman got a new lease on life. Painted in Ipswich red, white, and black, eight taps were added and it became an instant hit.

Inspired, the brewery gave the same treatment to a 1951 Ford F-1, known as "Big Red" (three taps), and a 1948 Dodge Route Van, one of only thirty-nine models ever made, which is called "the Shag" (eight taps). As of the writing of this book a fourth tapmobile named Wallace was being added to the fleet. "There is something about old vehicles that make people smile, and when we bring them to parties and events, they are showstoppers," said Martin.

Bringing the tapmobiles to various events has led to yet another facet of this brewery's story: old-time baseball. A local club that plays by original rules asked the brewery to come by and pour during games. Guys from the brewery took such a shine to the old ways that they formed their own club, Brewers of Ipswich Base Ball Club. Composed of all the brewery employees, Martin said they aren't great (other teams have players who competed at the high school and college levels), but they sure do have a good time. They even played at a recent tournament in Cooperstown, New York.

There is so much to Ipswich that Martin said it's more than a job, but rather a lifestyle.

Ipswich Ale Brewery

Opened: 1991.

Owner: Rob Martin.

Brewer: Dan Lipke, head brewer.

System: 30-barrel self-made, 60-barrel Santa Rosa.

Production: 21,000 barrels in 2011.

Tours: Call for times.

Take-out beer: Growlers.

Extras: Happy hour. Live music. Tapmobiles.

Special considerations: Handicapped-accessible.

Parking: On site.

Other area beer sites:

- **Choate Bridge Pub** (3 South Main St., Ipswich, 978-356-2931, www.choate bridgepub.com) is a comfortable corner bar downtown. Solid bar food and good taps, including Ipswich brands, make it a good spot for a night out.
- **The 1640 Hart House** (51 Linebrook Road, Ipswich, 978-356-1640, www.1640 harthouse.com) is a quaint tavern with an inspired menu. Reservations are recommended.
- **The Black Cow** (16 Bay Road, South Hamilton, 978-468-1166, www.blackcow restaurants.com) has a great tap list that includes state favorites, such as Ipswich, Harpoon, and Wachusett, as well as other well-known craft brands.

Lowell Beer Works

203 Cabot Street, Lowell, MA 01854
978-937-2337 • www.beerworks.net

When you get out of the confines of a city, you tend to have the luxury of more space. Compared to its sister locations in Boston, the Lowell Beer Works is almost palatial. First there is a large patio space, spread with tables and shade umbrellas, leading to the main entrance. Inside, there is a large bar and to the left a spacious dining room, where patrons are fortunate to have a view into the impressive production brewery that produces much of this local chain's output.

The first time we visited the Lowell Beer Works it was July and the temperature was 100 degrees. The patio was empty, save for one couple lounging at a table in the shade and eagerly imbibing watermelon ales, complete with a fresh triangular slice of the real fruit as a garnish. It was immediately appealing.

Intentionally or not, this was the best type of advertising: subliminal. Consider the Widmer Brothers of Oregon who are credited with creating the unfiltered American wheat beer style. When it was first unleashed on the Portland beer scene in the early 1980s, wait staff at pubs would just walk through the crowds with trays of the hazy golden unfiltered beer. It enticed enough people to try it once, making them return customers afterwards. It's similar to how the best advertisement for Guinness is seeing a properly poured pint, with the cascading carbonation turning into a perfectly fluffy white head, being placed in front of the customer next to you at the bar.

By the time we got to the bar, watermelon was the only thing on the brain. When the glass arrived, with that perfect wedge of ripened juicy fruit, the experience was sublime. Refreshing and, despite the use of fruit extract, the summer fruit flavor was not overwhelming. It was subtle with the malt and hops coming into play, but not too much. In all, it was balanced. Watermelon, we believe, is one of the rites of summer, a perfect pleasure. Taking a bite, the fresh fruit had absorbed some of the beer flavor, enhancing both and bringing the whole thing alive with a pop. When done with the fruit, there is no shame in putting the rind back into the glass and finishing off the beer with a floating garnish.

Size aside, the Lowell location looks similar to the other Beer Works locations. It has a modern industrial feel with brushed metal, exposed rivets, HVAC piping, brick, and cool wood tones. The menu is similar as well, with fist-sized burgers, flatbread pizzas, and meat and potato fare.

It is important to note that there is a second bar in this building called the Brewery Exchange. While not owned by Beer Works, they are just as fun, because on Thursday through Saturday nights they turn on their mechanical bull for those brave, stupid, or both.

The fact that Beer Works is a chain has led some beer enthusiasts and purists to decry what flows from their taps. This is a mistake, because under the supervision of revered brewer Tim Morse and the capable brewing of Herb Lindveit (who runs the Lowell location), Beer

Beers Brewed: Bunker Hill Blueberry Ale, Shawsheen Light, Merrimack Golden, Lowell Pale Ale, Boston Common, Dye House IPA, Spindle City Red, Boott's Nut Brown Ale, Curley's Irish Stout, and a rotating variety of seasonal and specialty beers.

The Pick: This brewery likes to put fruit and vegetables into beer, and the Habanero Stout uses the real thing, giving the ale a spicy hot nose and finish. Brave quaffers will go for a second round, but one is plenty.

Works is an example of what to do right when it comes to introducing a new customer base to beers, while staying true to tradition.

It was a comfort to see one employee, Paul Alphen, walk two new customers expertly through the beer offerings, suggesting beers that were "similar to," but far superior to the mass-marketed brews being asked for. It was even more comforting to eavesdrop and hear that the customers were summarily impressed and even ordered a second round.

Lowell Beer Works

Opened: 2001.

Owner: Joe Slesar.

Brewers: Herb Lindtviet, Rich Ferrell, and Derek Wasak.

System: 40-barrel DME.

Production: 30,000 barrels capacity

Hours: Daily, 11:30 A.M. to 1 A.M.

Tours: Upon request.

Take-out beer: Growlers and six-packs.

Special consideration: Handicapped-accessible.

Parking: On-street parking.

The Tap/Haverhill Brewery

100 Washington Street, Haverhill, MA 01832
978-374-1117 • www.tapbrewpub.com

The elevator doors slid open onto the ground floor and there, inexplicably and absurdly in front of us, was a koi pond. The space that currently serves as the fermentation and bottling-line room for the Haverhill Brewery once housed an antique store and the owners wanted something to enhance the ambiance for customers. When the antiques moved out, it just made sense to keep the golden and black koi that called the stone pool home, explained brewer Jon Curtis. So the fish stayed and feeding and caring for them became the responsibility of an assistant brewer.

The fermentation room is next door to the actual brewhouse, bar, and restaurant and connected to the rig by 150 feet of stainless steel piping. It is a jerry-rigged system that works for this brewery. The bar is currently known as The Tap and has been around (with various names and themes) since 1897. It is one in a strip of buildings that was destroyed during a fire in the early 1890s. The post-industrial town of Haverhill was once famous for the manufacturing of women's shoes and now, as the third-largest city in the state, serves as a commuter town for the Boston workforce and a thriving artist community.

Beers Brewed: Leather Lips IPA, Homerun APA, Haver-Ale, Whittier White, Gestalt, Triskelion, Three Graces, Snowbound, La Dame de Peronne, Joshua Norton, Ascension, Beerstand Berlinerweiss.

The Pick: Beerstand Berlinerweiss is a rare find at brewpubs. Curtis achieves the acidic tartness from sourmashing and the result is a great sipping beer.

It's a great neighborhood spot where even first-time visitors who tread across the plank wood floor are treated like regulars by bartender Tom Amante. The decor is an eclectic theme that feels like it would work well in a Sherlock Holmes novel. Various antiques and other knickknacks fit into nooks and crevices. Bookshelves in the dining area are lined with leather-bound encyclopedias and Massachusetts law books that are aging gracefully.

The dining room lends itself to conversation and is a delight in the cooler months. But, in the summer, head out to the spacious wooden deck in the back. Sweeping views of the Merrimack River beg patrons to order another round, watch the boats slide by, and tap their Florsheims along with local bands who regularly perform. On a far railing, hops have stretched from the soil one story below and curl around wooden beams.

People come for the ambiance, but also the beer. Since it first opened as a brewery in 2003, it has been home to a number of brewers who have since gone onto other brewing adventures. Their departures cleared the way for Curtis, a Haverhill native. When he came on board, he inherited three recipes—the HaverAle, the Leatherlips IPA, and the Whittier White.

The brews Curtis introduced showcase his passion and talent for German lagers. His Gestalt, a hoppy altbier, won gold at the Great American Beer Festival in 2010 and is now a year-round offering. He also produces a black lager, Indian Schwarzbier, and the tart Beerstand Berlinerweiss. There are rotating seasonals and experiments that can be found on tap. Downstairs from the bar, next to the game room, are craggy-walled rooms containing the fermentation tanks. Despite modern equipment, the room gives the beer a traditional feel, a callback to the days when beer was lagered in caves, and it adds to the depth of flavor in Curtis's beers.

Overall, Curtis calls The Tap a brewpub with a distributing habit. From the basement space—with the koi pond—a steady line of 12- and 22-ounce bottles are filled, labeled, loaded, and shipped throughout the commonwealth and into northern Rhode Island. Most of what goes out the door in 12-ounce bottles are ales, while the 22-ounce bottles get the German lager variations. The labels are easily distinguishable on shelves: the lager features pictures of shoe outlines, once used by cobblers in the city.

The smaller bottles are pasted with the drawings of pinup models designed by artist Jessica Dougherty, whose fiery red-haired image graces the Leatherlips label. Those sometimes racy images have led to some pretty intense hate mail, said Curtis. One two-page letter from "a children's book author" took particular offense to the HaverAle label on which a woman in a halter top shows off quite a bit of skin. It doesn't help matters that the particular style is cream ale, the author pointed out. Sexist or not, the beer inside the bottles is solid and worth a regular place in any beer drinker's rotation.

The Tap hosts a well-attended and quite fun beer festival each fall, usually in September. It provides a great opportunity to try some of Curtis's offerings that are not always available (he was aging a lambic when we last visited), along with those from other breweries from the area.

It may sound like a cliché, but in keeping with the shoe theme, run, don't walk to The Tap. You won't be disappointed.

The Tap/Haverhill Brewery

Opened: 2003.

Owner: John Fahimian.

Brewers: Jon Curtis and Brian Davis.

System: 3-vessel Century system with mash/kettle tank and lauter tun.

Production: 1,500 barrels in 2011.

Hours: Tuesday through Saturday, 11:30 A.M. to last call; Sunday, noon to last call.

Take-out beer: Growlers, six-packs, 22-oz. bottles.

Tours: By appointment.

Extras: Live music. Pool tables. Large deck overlooking Merrimack River.

Special considerations: Handicapped-accessible. Located across the street from commuter rail stop.

Parking: Lot behind the building and a parking garage one block away.

Other area beer sites:

- **The Grill Next Door** (653 Broadway, Haverhill, 978-241-7337, www.thegrill nextdoor.net) boasts an impressive craft beer list and a solid menu of burgers and the like.

RiverWalk Brewing Company

36 Main Street, Amesbury, MA 01913
978-489-9230 • www.riverwalkbrewing.com

With a name like RiverWalk, one might expect this brewery to be in San Antonio, home to the famous, well, River Walk. But the bedroom community of Amesbury is just as suitable. In fact, just outside the brewery wall is the Powow River, which runs into the Merrimack River.

The Main Street address may seem familiar to sharp-eyed readers. That's because the old mill building that houses RiverWalk—one of the state's newest breweries—is also the home of Cody Brewing. Steve Sanderson leases space in a rear corner of Cody Brewing, which not only helped with licensing requirements, but also gives customers a two-for-one experience. That's because the breweries are producing different styles of beer.

We met Sanderson on a Saturday morning when he was still working on his pilot system, a homebrew rig he largely put together himself. He busied himself running hoses, igniting burners, and quickly shutting off others. The wit beer he was working on became more floral with each addition.

Sanderson plans to stay small for a while, although he wants to eventually upgrade to a 10-barrel system. His current 2-barrel brewhouse will crank out just three styles of beer: the Belgian-style ale known as Gnomad, an English bitter called Uncle Bob's, and the River-Walk IPA. The plan is for draft accounts and 22-ounce bottles.

"One reason to stay small is because I want to capture the traditions of Europe, where you get fresh ale, like on cask, that is to be enjoyed quickly," Sanderson told us.

He was spoiled on good beer early on. During a visit to the Czech Republic nearly two decades ago, he discovered fresh pilsner. Upon returning home he began to seek out better beer wherever he could find it. That included visits to many beer festivals, which had its fortuitous side as well, since he met his now wife at one. Eventually he took the route of so many others and began brewing at home. Now, as he starts his next venture, he

Beers Brewed: Gnomad, Uncle Bob's Bitter, River-Walk IPA.

The Pick: Uncle Bob's Bitter is the perfect pub beer. Smooth with a little bite, it lends itself to the feeling of a cozy English bar with hearty food at the table, surrounded by good company.

wants to take the sensibilities of those European breweries and stay close to home, serving his specific community. Expansion comes later. "Freshness and quality above all else," he said.

RiverWalk Brewing Company

Opened: 2010.

Owners: Steve and Betsy Sanderson.

Brewers: Steve Sanderson and Evan Jesperson.

System: Custom-built, direct-fire 2-barrel system.

Production: 200 barrels in 2011.

Tours: Call or email for information.

Take-out beer: Growlers.

Parking: Plenty on street.

Other area beer sites:

- **Ale House** (33 Main Street, Amesbury, 978-388-1950, www.amesburyalehouse .com) has an excellent selection of beer, one of the best north of Boston.
- **The Barking Dog** (21 Friend Street, Amesbury, 978-388-9537, www.barkingdog grill.com) offers a more relaxed, publike atmosphere for a few pints.
- **Phat Cats Bistro** (65A Market Street, Amesbury, 978-388-2777, www.phatcats bistro.com) has a smaller beer selection than the two above, but makes up for it with amazing food, a solid wine list, and fresh oysters.

Cody Brewing Company

36 Main Street, Amesbury, MA 01913
978-378-3424 • www.codybrewing.com

When we met Sean Cody, he was experiencing a period in his brewery's history that he described as "one step forward and two steps back." Having run into unforeseen hiccups, his attorney had advised him to disconnect his 7-barrel brewing system. So, there it stood in pieces, as if it had just been moved in and was waiting to get down to business. It will be hooked up again, said Cody. In the meantime, he is contracting brewing facilities at the Mercury Brewing Company and handling all the recipes and bottling while things get sorted out.

The self-named brewery is Sean's second venture into the brewing world. In 2005, he opened a brew-your-own shop in Danvers that also sold homebrewing supplies. It was a successful venture and after a year, Cody got the necessary licensing to make his own beer for distribution. He sent his Amber, Stout, and White Ale out into the world, where it was well received. The year after, Cody took a leap of faith, closed the BYO part of the business, and opened a bar in its place. The Cody Alehouse, he told us, was a great chance to experiment with different beers and expand offerings. Helped by Chris Gendron, who goes by the nickname "Gee Man," Cody was able to get a variety of beers into eager hands.

However, not all was well in Danvers, and after some back and forth with the town, Cody was forced to shut down in 2009. He spent some time looking around for a new home and settled on the water-centric town of Amesbury. The address is Main Street, but the brewery is actually down an alley, opposite the Powwow River, which runs into the Merrimack.

Cody plans to open again soon in a mill, powered by the river, and turn this into a comfortable customer experience. There is a patio next to the flowing Powwow, perfect for a few tables and chairs, a great spot to sit and enjoy a beer. They will also lease space inside to new upstart RiverWalk Brewing Company. For now, if you want to enjoy a Cody beer, a list of shops and bars where it's available is on their website.

Cody is active in the Massachusetts Brewers Guild and brings an infectious optimism to not only his brewery, but the industry overall. We wish him the best of luck getting back into his space and putting more beer on tap.

Beers Brewed: S.O.S., Cody's Pub Ale, Gee Man's Lemon Honey Hypnotic Tonic, Powow, Wheelers Brown, Cody's Original North Shore Amber Ale, Black Hole Stout, No Name IPA, Dog Daze.

The Pick: Gee Man's Lemon Honey Hypnotic Tonic is a strong ale that gets a bright kick from generous amounts of honey (1 pound per gallon) and what the brewery describes as "an obscene amount of citrus." It's a gentle 8.8 percent monster that deserves careful consideration.

Cody Brewing Company

Opened: 2005.
Owner: Sean Cody.
Brewers: Sean Cody and Chris "Gee Man" Gendron.
System: 7-barrel custom-built system
Production: 525 barrels in 2011.

Tours: Call for an appointment.

Take-out beer: Not available

Extras: Homebrew Nights.

Special considerations: Handicapped-accessible.

Parking: On street.

Other area beer sites: See list under RiverWalk Brewing Company, page 95.

Massachusetts Contract Breweries

The idea of a contract brewery is not a new one, but has certainly become more popular in recent years. Brewers without a place of their own can lease out equipment and space from an existing brewery and release beers under their own name. When he first started Samuel Adams, Jim Koch contract brewed, and without the overhead of a brick-and-mortar structure, it freed him up to sell more beer and spend more money on marketing.

As more brewers seek to start their own business, they are turning to that model and hanging a shingle inside another's building. Not all brewers are hands on, however. Some contract brewers will go to a brewery with a concept or a name and ask them to create a recipe, brew it, and package it. Those owners have little to do with the creative process outside of selling. That's not to say the beer is not worth your time or dollars. Remember the brewers who make contract beer are talented, dedicated professionals who don't want you drinking rubbish.

For the purpose of this section, we are focusing on contract breweries that have offices in Massachusetts only and use one of the contract breweries in the state. There are others that are headquartered in the commonwealth but brew at facilities in neighboring states. We enjoy many of those beers, but in the interest of keeping the book about Massachusetts, we'll focus on the brewers below.

There are three major contract brewers in the state: Mercury Brewing Company in Ipswich, Paper City in Holyoke, and Just Beer in Westport. Some other breweries do small work for other brewers but these three are the major players and where the majority of contract brewing is done for in-state entities.

So, if you're drinking one of these contract brews, you're supporting a local business and still getting a quality beer.

- **Notch Brewing** (www.notchsession.com). Chris Lohring is no stranger to the Massachusetts brewing scene. He was at the now-gone Atlantic Coast Brewing (often referred to as Tremont Brewery) and knows the blood, sweat, and tears that go into running a brewery. After a breather, he's returned to the fold and has gone in a new direction—the session beer. All of his beers are 4.5 percent ABV or less. This is a dramatic shift from many brewers who try to cram as much alcohol into their beers as possible. With the Notch beers (named after the way people keep track of things) you can have a few without feeling like you've been hit by a train. We love it!

- **Pretty Things Beer and Ale Project** (www.prettythingsbeertoday .com). Dann and Martha Paquette do not call this venture a contract brewery. They think of themselves as gypsy brewers, but more than that, a project. Dann is a brewer with a long and distinguished résumé, having spent time in more than a half dozen breweries. The flagship beer, Jack D'Or, is an American saison, and other offerings include Baby Tree, a 9 percent quadruple, and Fluffy White Rabbits, which is "some sort of triple," according to Dann. While they are not out to create new styles, they do enjoy playing around with the established ones. Lucky us!

- **Clown Shoes Beer** (www.clownshoesbeer.com). With their quirky and sometimes risqué labels, Clown Shoes has been gaining headlines and fans with its various beers. "Our mission now is to produce beer without pretension, while being free and a little crazy," is how they describe the feeling behind brews like Tramp Stamp, Lubrication, and Happy Feet. The brewery name was originally submitted to Beer Advocate as the potential name for a collaboration beer with Dogfish Head Ales. When Clown Shoes didn't even crack the top five, the fellas behind it decided to go their own way. We're glad they did, because they are making some fine beer.

- **Concord Brewery** (www.drinkrapscallion.com). Since its formation in the 1990s, Concord has been through a few incarnations and a few owners. Along the way it has picked up some world-class recipes, thanks to a bit of history and some talented brewers who came through the doors. Originally located in an actual brewery in Concord, the beers are now brewed at both Paper City and Pioneer under the Rapscallion label. The draft-only offerings include Belgian-inspired brews from Dann Paquette, who served as a brewer long ago, and a lager recipe from the long-departed Harvard Brewing Company, dating to 1898.

- **Sherwood Forest Brewers** (www.sherwoodbrewers.com). With a quartet of beers named after the Robin Hood stories, these mostly English-inspired ales are available throughout New England.

- **Backlash Beer Company** (www.backlashbeer.com). Helder Pimentel was a homebrewer who saw the success that other contract brewers were having and decided to give it a go. "I think it was one of those things where you have this dream in your head and once you started to get that confirmation from external sources that you're not out of your mind, you go for it," he told us. "And that's basically what we did." The beers have a Belgian influence to them, but appeal to both the seasoned beer drinker and the new-to-craft crowd.

- **Blatant Brewery** (www.blatantbrewery.com). Here's another brewery started by a veteran Massachusetts brewer. Matthew Steinberg is the force behind Blatant. Already armed with an impressive résumé, he was ready to head out on his own. Using the equipment at Just Beer in Westport, he is running the gamut. There is a 6.5 percent IPA, a 3.9 percent session ale, and a 9.5 percent stout.

- **Frosty Knuckle** (www.frostyknuckle.com). From former business partners at Cape Ann Brewing comes this contract brewery that's currently producing one beer—Frosty Knuckle Ale. It is named with a nod towards an old maritime story about a man who was separated from his ship and spent five days at sea in winter, holding onto the oars of his rowboat. When frostbite claimed the man's fingers he gave up a life at sea and opened a tavern.

- **Somerville Brewing Company** (www.slumbrew.com). Recipes are developed inside a 350-square-foot nanobrewery on Caitlin Jewell and Jeff Leiter's property. After extensive refinement, the beers of Somerville Brewing Company's Slumbrew brand are produced at Ipswich. Jewell and Leiter developed their recipes after traveling to some of the world's great beer destinations.

- **High & Mighty Beer Company** (www.highandmightybeer.com). Spearheaded by Will Shelton, of the famed beer-importing family Shelton Brothers, who have brought many great beers to our shores, High & Mighty makes European styles, but with an American flair, generally with low alcohol. Will tells us that he is very keen to promote lower ABV beers as part of healthful living and he is passionately against the glorification of excess in brewing, especially where alcohol is concerned.

The Greater Boston Area

The greater Boston area is the heart and soul of Massachusetts and where the vast majority of the state's residents put down roots. It's made up of the city of Boston itself, of course, as well as the surrounding regions, such as Cambridge, Somerville, and others. In fact, the greater Boston area as a whole is made up of eighty-three cities and towns and is home to more than four million people.

By contrast, the actual city of Boston is almost petite, with only about 617,000 residents living within its compact borders. But that's the way the locals like it. It's a great mid-sized city, both manageable and homey, but also overflowing with historic significance, fabulous architecture, cultural attractions, and top-notch restaurants and nightlife.

Boston is deeply unique and interesting because of its juxtapositions. Sleek skyscrapers rise towards the clouds just blocks from seventeenth-century houses, steepled churches, and twisty streets lined with antique gas lamps. It also has a reputation of being a little more European than other American cities, with many leafy parks, waterfront areas for wandering, great outdoor cafes, and a plethora of rowdy Irish pubs filled to the brim with passionate (some might even say crazy) sports fans.

Whether you're a local or a visitor, it's important to have good walking shoes. This compact city is a wanderer's paradise, and the best way to appreciate its dynamic neighborhoods is on foot. Although the subway system, called The T, is great, you will without question have to spend time walking around under your own steam to explore properly.

Boston was originally settled in 1630 and named by several prominent Puritans after their hometown back in England. It had a great location on a deep, sheltered bay, and soon a bustling economy based on shipbuilding, fishing, whaling, and trading began to flourish. Puritans flooded into the area and soon Boston became the capital of the Massachusetts Bay Colony, and shortly thereafter the wealthiest and most influential city in the New World. But as important as business was to Boston, it was also founded on strictly religious roots, brought in by the Puritans seeking freedom from religious persecution in England. In fact, Harvard College's original mission, dated 1636, was to "prepare young men to be ministers."

By the latter half of the eighteenth century, animosity towards mother England was growing high, with resentment building over what colonists saw as unnecessary taxation laws. This mutual frustration led to uprisings by local colonists, ending in famous events such as the Boston Massacre of 1770, when five protesting locals were shot and killed by British soldiers, and the Boston Tea Party, when angry Sons of Liberty dramatically dumped 342 chests of tea from British trading ships directly into Boston Harbor as a sign of protest. Shortly thereafter the two regions were embroiled in the Revolutionary War, with British troops arriving in Boston Harbor and marching from the city to Lexington and Concord, where the war itself began.

Once the war ended, Boston quickly went back to the business of business, with fishing, whaling, and trade continuing to dominate its economy. Boston was later overthrown in terms of economic importance by the exploding population centers of nearby Philadelphia and New York. But at the same time, the city was also rising in terms of intellectual importance, becoming famous for its world-class universities, fine art, culture, and stunning architecture.

Boston is now known for being an inherently livable place, with intellectual energy and creativity brought in by the many thousands of students that descend upon the city each fall. It's highly popular with tourists, who visit in droves to take in the history, architecture, culture, and nightlife, but it is even more fiercely loved by locals, who find that the mix of history and big-city mentality creates a wonderful atmosphere to live and work in.

Like any other major American city, finding a great place to stay within the city limits of Boston is going to be on the pricey side unless you do a little sleuthing. Here are some interesting options.

- **John Jeffries House** (www.johnjeffrieshouse.com) in the Beacon Hill neighborhood is a bed-and-breakfast with atmosphere that is within walking distance of many major attractions.

- **Harborside Inn of Boston** (www.harborsideinnboston.com), a European-style boutique hotel originally built in 1846 as a mercantile shipping warehouse, is further downtown.

- **The Fairmont Copley Plaza** (www.fairmont.com/copleyplaza) is the place to go if money is no object. It's a luxury hotel that drips with elegance, featuring shiny marble and the kind of chandeliers that will make your jaw drop.

- **A Bed and Breakfast in Cambridge** (www.cambridgebnb.com) is located in Cambridge just two blocks from Harvard Yard. This 1897 colonial house has just three rooms (and a shared bathroom), but with great period details and welcoming hospitality.

- **The Charles Hotel** (www.charleshotel.com) in Cambridge is pure luxury, with sweeping views of the Charles River and a reputation for welcoming high-end travelers from all over the world.

Boston is a city of neighborhoods, and each one is distinct and worthy of exploration. The main touristy areas are in what locals refer to as "downtown." If you consider Boston Common, the city park, to be the heart of town, the surrounding neighborhoods around it are generally the most popular. While it would be impossible to list all of Boston's many attractions in this book, we'll do our best to recommend the top highlights, organized by neighborhood.

The best way to orient yourself to the city is with the absolutely touristy but still interesting **Freedom Trail** (www.thefreedomtrail.org), a connection of sixteen historic sites in downtown Boston, all linked together with a red-painted brick line. The trail stretches for two and a half miles from Boston Common to the Bunker Hill Monument and can be self-guided or taken as a tour led by a costumed actor, who will explain the sites as you pass. It's a great way to take in a couple of Boston's famous neighborhoods, soak up a little atmosphere, and learn about the region's astounding history all at once.

A great place for wandering is Beacon Hill (www.beaconhillonline.com), a quintessentially Boston neighborhood with a village feel, made up of beautiful redbrick townhouses, gas lamps lit twenty-four hours a day, lush parks, and meandering cobblestone streets. This is a wealthy residential neighborhood, and wonderful for taking a stroll on a nice day.

- **Boston Common** (www.cityofboston.gov/freedomtrail/bostoncommon.asp) is nearly fifty acres of gently rolling parklands in the heart of Boston's downtown. Originally created in 1634 as a sheep and cow pasture, this park is now the heart of Boston, with options for ice-skating at Frog Pond in winter, concerts or Shakespeare in the Park at the Francis Parkman Bandstand in summer, or simply a great place to take a stroll or do some people-watching from a comfortable bench any time of the year.

The Downtown Crossing neighborhood is primarily a commercial district.

- **Faneuil Hall Marketplace** (www.faneuilhallmarketplace.com) is a landmark public building that was constructed in 1742 and comprises a downstairs food market and upstairs meeting hall from the early days of the Revolution. Originally known by the nickname "Cradle of Liberty," it's now a place to buy Boston-based goods or souvenirs and listen to talks offered by National Park Service rangers about the building's historic significance.

- **Quincy Marketplace**, directly behind Faneuil Hall, was originally a collection of fish warehouses. It was transformed in the 1970s into a pedestrian mall, modeled after London's Covent Garden, with boutique shopping, street performers, and a bustling food court made up of stalls from local Boston restaurants. The area is packed with tourists at any given moment, but is still a pleasant place for a snack and a stroll.

Another great area for wandering is the North End (www.northend boston.com), Boston's congested and charming neighborhood that is chock-full of Italian restaurants, grocers, and pastry shops. This neighborhood was home to an influx of Italian immigrants in the early 1900s, and although it's now home to many young professionals seeking an easy commute to the Financial District, it still retains Old World charm and delicious food options. No visit to Boston would be complete without a stop for a pastry or gelato on Hanover Street.

- **The Paul Revere House** (www.paulreverehouse.org) in the North End neighborhood was the home of the silversmith who became legendary for his 1775 ride to warn patriot militia of the British approach before the Battles of Lexington and Concord. Actually the oldest house still standing in the city, it was originally built in 1680 and is a National Historic Landmark.

An absolutely unbeatable area for killing an afternoon is The Back Bay (www.visitbostonbackbay.com/site) a sophisticated neighborhood with shopping, galleries, and fine dining. The heart of the area is Copley Square, a large plaza where classical music concerts are held in the spring and summer months.

- **Boston Public Library** (www.bpl.org/central), established in 1848, was the first free public library in the country. The Central Library has been in Copley Square in the building designed by Charles Follen McKim since 1895. It was expanded with a second building, designed by Philip Johnson, in 1972. This location serves as the headquarters for the BPL library system.

- **Public Garden** (www.cityofboston.gov/parks/emerald/public_garden.asp) is a beautiful outdoor park space and location of America's first public botanical garden, as well as home of the famous Swan Boats (www.swanboats.com), which are docked in the park's center lagoon.

- **Newbury Street** (www.newbury-st.com) is eight blocks of shopping, especially noted for its hair salons, fashion boutiques, and high-end restaurants.

For sports lovers, what trip to Boston would be complete without a visit to Fenway? While the neighborhood itself doesn't seem to have a lot to recommend it at first glance, it's got some great attractions lurking under the surface.

- **Fenway Park** (www.redsox.com), home of the Boston Red Sox, is a great attraction, not only for taking in a baseball game but also for a ballpark tour.

- **Museum of Fine Arts Boston** (www.mfa.org), with more than 450,000 works in its collection, is one of the most beloved fine arts museums in the country.

- **Isabella Stewart Gardner Museum** (www.gardnermuseum.org) is also chock-full of priceless American and European paintings.

While exploring Boston, don't forget the most advantageous view of all—by sea. Take a Boston Harbor Cruise (www.bostonharborcruises.com) to enjoy the skyline from the peaceful vantage point of the water, or be a little goofier and join up on a Boston Duck Tour (www.bostonducktours.com), where you'll take in the views from aboard a World War II–era vehicle that morphs from city streets to floating along the Charles River.

While you're feeling watery, take some time to explore the Seaport District, home to several fascinating museums.

- The long-shuttered **Boston Tea Party Ship and Museum** (www.bostonteapartyship.com) is on track to reopen in late June 2012.

- **Institute of Contemporary Art** (www.icaboston.org).

- **Boston Children's Museum** (www.bostonchildrensmuseum.org).

The South End is listed in the National Register of Historic Places and known for its Victorian architecture. You'll find lots of shopping, galleries, markets, and fine dining.

- **Mapparium** (www.marybakereddylibrary.org/exhibits/mapparium), located within the Christian Science Center in the South End neighborhood, is a unique attraction. Here, you'll stand on a bridge located inside of a three-story painted glass globe created in 1935. With varying displays and light shows demonstrating the changing nature of the geography and global history of the planet, this display in gorgeous stained glass is absolutely unforgettable.

Don't forget to head outside of Boston proper into the venerable and beautiful city of Cambridge (www.cambridge-usa.org), just across the Charles River. Here, you can wander Harvard Square and its swarm of shops, restaurants, and bookstores, explore the campuses of Harvard University (www.harvard.edu) and Massachusetts Institute of Technology (www.mit.edu), or just people-watch from one of many sidewalk cafes. Spend some time visting the many squares in the area—Inman, Kendall, and Porter, to name just a few—or head into nearby Somerville (www.somervillema.com) to walk around and take in the atmosphere of this vibrant community. Also plan to stop at these museums.

- **Harvard Museum of Natural History** (www.hmnh.harvard.edu).

- **Harvard Art Museum** (www.artmuseums.harvard.edu).

For more information on traveling in Boston in general, including accommodation options, we recommend the websites www.mass vacation.com and www.bostonusa.com. There's no shortage of sites and great experiences, and we wish you happy travels throughout all of Beantown.

Finally, here's a list of some area beer sites to check out.

- **Lower Depths** (476 Commonwealth Avenue #1, Boston, 617-266-6662) is one of our favorite bars in the city. Comfortably close to Fenway, with knowledgeable staff and a rotating tap selection, no one ever leaves disappointed.

- **Deep Ellum** (477 Cambridge Street, Allston, 617-787-2337, www.deepellum-boston.com) has great beer and a wonderful menu to boot.

- **Sunset Grill** (130 Brighton Ave, Allston, 617-254-1331, www.allstons finest.com) has a dizzying selection of taps in a fun atmosphere.

- **Lord Hobo** (92 Hampshire St., Cambridge 617-250-8454, www.lord hobo.com) is a favorite spot for a nightcap, or an all-nighter.

- **Cambridge Common** (1667 Massachusetts, Cambridge, 617-547-1228, www.cambridgecommonrestaurant.com) offers a lot of local beers in an upscale college atmosphere.

- **The Publick House Beer Bar and Kitchen** (1648 Beacon St., Brookline, 617-277-2880).

- **Bukowski's Tavern** (50 Dalton St., Boston, 617-427-9999, http://bukowskitavern.net/cambridge).

- **Redbones Barbeque** (55 Chester St., Somerville, 617-628-2200).

Boston Beer Works Fenway

61 Brookline Avenue, Boston, MA 02215
617-536-2337 • www.beerworks.net

Boston is an incredible sports town. While most of New England lays claim and pledges allegiance to the Red Sox, Patriots, Bruins, and Celtics, the fans in Boston seem to root louder, defend stronger, and celebrate in a more unabashed fashion when the teams win titles, which has been the case in recent years.

As is true with players, stadiums, too, come and go. There has been one constant, however, and that is the temple known as Fenway Park. The home of the Red Sox, hard against the Mass Pike, is where fans saw their hopes dashed for the eighty-six-year period in which they failed to win a World Series, something blamed on the Curse of the Bambino, after the Sox traded Babe Ruth to the reviled New York Yankees, and where their dreams soared when they took the world championship in 2004 and again in 2007.

Directly across the street from Fenway is another of the city's great passions, something in which it truly excels: a brewery. Specifically a Boston Beer Works, the first to open in the city, one that is now part of a statewide chain of breweries.

Beers Brewed: Bunker Hill Blueberry Ale, Hub Light, Baker's Island Blond, Mayflower Maybock, Fenway American Pale Ale, Boston Common, Back Bay IPA, Victory Red, Beantown Nut Brown Ale, Curley's Irish Stout, and a rotating variety of seasonal and specialty beers.

The Pick: Of course it is going to be the Fenway American Pale Ale. It's got the aggressive hop flavor that suits serious fans. It tastes like victory!

Joe Slesar and his brother, Steve, started Boston Beer Works in 1992. They found instant success, according to those who were there at the time brewing house-made beers for the Fenway faithful, as well as making a big range of beers for locals in the off-season. A location was added in Salem in 1995. The company's beer continues to be distributed to three Beer Works locations inside Logan Airport. In 2007, Joe became the sole owner of the company and embarked on an expansion plan for Beer Works that included opening locations in Lowell, Hingham, and the second Boston location on Canal Street near the TD Garden arena.

At the Fenway location, well-trained staff knows how to sling pints quickly, keep crowding at the bar to a minimum, and get people into seats by the first pitch. Food comes out hot and fast and pints are cold and flavorful.

While this Beer Works might not yet have the history of its famous Green Monster neighbor, it's a perfect place to grab a few beers before the game, after the game, during the game, and even on nongame days.

Boston Beer Works Fenway

Opened: 1992.
Owner: Joe Slesar.
Brewers: Jon Morse and Clark Van Vliet.
System: 15-barrel DME.
Production: 1,800 barrels in 2011.
Hours: Daily, 11:30 A.M. to 1 A.M.
Tours: By request.
Take-out beer: Growlers and six-packs.
Special considerations: Handicapped-accessible.
Parking: On street.

Boston Beer Works Canal Street

112 Canal Street, Boston, MA 02114
617-896-2337 • www.beerworks.net

When the doors open here on a typical day at lunchtime, the location is packed full of suits from neighborhood office buildings, grabbing a quick bite to eat. As the afternoon goes on, that crowd gives way to regulars, stopping in for a quick afternoon pint. After 5, the crowd swells with the after-work folks, with ties askew and jackets slung casually on the backs of chairs. If it's a game night—the TD Garden is one block over—Bruins or Celtics fans gather for some pregame activity. On the weekends, families come in for brunch, and cartoons replace ESPN on the TVs. There's a time for everyone at Boston Beer Works Canal Street.

"We want it to be a place where people can come, have great beer, a good time, and then go back to the real world," explained Tim Morse, director of brewing operations for the group of Beer Works locations scattered throughout the eastern part of the state. Morse, a brewing veteran who worked for the famed Anchor Brewery back in the 1970s, has a wealth of knowledge that he continues to pass on to the brewers now employed by the chain.

Given their tourist-minded location, Beer Works makes sure that they educate those still unaccustomed to craft beer. This includes a handy color-coded chart that shows beers on tap from lightest to darkest. It helps in a pinch when the bar is packed. There are regular beers on tap, such as a light lager, an IPA, a stout, and an amber ale. But there are also seasonal beers that come on tap regularly each month and often match a rotating food menu. Plus, beers brewed at other Beer Works locations find their way to sister breweries, ensuring that each visit brings the promise of a varied selection. Samplers, four beers at a time, are popular here and come on a piece of paper with a pen to encourage customers to take notes to help them remember later what pleased their palates.

Beers Brewed: Bunker Hill Blueberry Ale, Hub Light, Baker's Island Blond, Haymarket Hefeweizen, Fenway American Pale Ale, Ben Nevis Triple IPA, Double Pale Ale, Victory Red, Beantown Nut Brown Ale, Buckeye Oatmeal Stout, and a rotating variety of seasonal and specialty beers.

The Pick: Pre-Prohibition Lager is crisp, malty, and hoppy and is a wonderful history lesson. Experience what earlier generations had access to and you'll find it's truly an inspired brew.

The education continues with the brewing system in full view and knowledgeable staff members who walk people through the grain-to-glass process.

Like others in the chain, Canal Street has a brushed-metal and wood-laminate décor, giving it an industrial feel that also manages to convey a sense of comfort. The menu is solid as well—American bar fare that reminds us in an age when white-linen restaurant cuisine is coming into vogue with beer that that there is still a place for a burger and fried pickles.

Boston Beer Works Canal Street

Opened: 2001.
Owner: Joe Slesar.
Brewers: Jim Carleton and Mcclean Hart.
System: 15-barrel JVNW.
Production: 1,900 barrels in 2011.
Hours: Daily, 11:30 A.M. to 1 A.M.
Tours: By request.
Take-out beer: Growlers and six-packs.
Special considerations: Handicapped-accessible.
Parking: On street.

Cambridge Brewing Company

Cambridge Brewing Co.

1 Kendall Square, Building 100,
Cambridge, MA 02139
617-494-1994 • www.cambridgebrewing.com

It doesn't take long for first-time visitors to notice the three large painted murals on the wall in the main area of this brew-pub. Depicted on the panels are regulars mixing with celebrities—real and cartoon—enjoying pints, a game of cards, and other vices in the very place you, the customer, are standing. Look around the room and it's likely you'll see some familiar faces in the flesh. One such person is depicted in the top left-hand corner of the panel to the left, owner Phil Bannatyne. In the mural, he's dressed like a sheriff, with a brown striped coat, a gold star on his lapel, a hat, and a bolo tie with the initials B. D. Later, I would come to know that stands for Brew Daddy.

"About fifteen years ago, an assistant brewer walked up to me, gave me a hug, and called me that," explained Bannatyne. "The name stuck, there is nothing more to the story than that. It was not a self-given nickname."

That mural, by the way, also depicts a young patron reading the book *Brewing for Beginners*, and it's a nice touch.

CBC makes the most of the space it has available. A brick patio in an office-complex courtyard leads into a casual dining area and the short bar. Skylights above the bar wash the room in light when weather conditions permit. A more formal, but not by much, dining room is in the back, sharing space with the mash tun and brew kettle. With this setup, brewer Will Meyers is usually in house and hard at work early—and done by the time the first customers arrive.

The pub has simple wooden floors and furnishings and a few stained glass panels of beer-filled pint glasses against various backdrops, which offer a pop of color in an otherwise minimalistic setting. Bannatyne said they succumbed to pressure and installed a TV after a few years of being open for business, but to date there is just one in the place, hanging over the bar. Given its location practically inside the MIT campus, Bannatyne said the crowd is more likely to gather to watch an announcement from Apple than a game.

Overall it's all about the conversation at this brewpub. Families, first dates, friends, and colleagues gather to relish the casual, clean atmosphere as knowledgeable staff deftly move from table to table, refreshing drinks and recommending dishes while seeming to be truly enjoying their place of work.

The menu has changed over the years, something Bannatyne said was due to wanting to do more than just keep the status quo. "We were making great beer—exceptional beer—and the food was just ordinary," he said. So, he brought in new staff and has watched the food progress from there. Much of what they serve is locally sourced from Massachusetts farms, including one in Concord. The kitchen also likes to use seafood caught in and around the harbor, giving seafood lovers a chance to taste day-of bounty.

Beers Brewed: Cambridge Amber, Charles River Porter, Regatta Golden, Tall Tale Pale Ale, Blackout Stout, Cerise Cassee, flower child i.p.a., Great Pumpkin Ale!, Kraftwerk, Valley Ghoul.

The Pick: Cambridge releases a barrel-aged summer barleywine called Arquebus, a 14 percent ABV brilliant genius of a beer. It is sherrylike, smooth, and boozy, with oak and grape, and stone fruit flavors play in perfect harmony. Sip and savor.

If you sit in the back dining room, watch as full plates emerge from the kitchen and return empty later. No leftovers in this crowd. Oh well. Just another reason to visit again and again.

Now, let's talk about the beers. Cambridge Brewing Company has a wealth of experience, being the third-oldest brewpub in the state (behind Northampton and the now defunct Commonwealth Brewing). It opened in the spring of 1989 and has worked continuously since then to not only perfect its recipes but also to break boundaries.

In 1990, after its then brewer visited Belgium, Cambridge was able to source a yeast strain and create its triple, which Bannatyne said was the first time a United States brewery created a Belgian-style beer. This claim was backed up by beer authority Michael Jackson.

Then came the barrels. After Meyers took the reins as brewer, they were clearing out some junk from the basement and the brewer asked Bannatyne if he could stash a few barrels there. "It has progressed ever since," said the owner. They now have fifty or so barrels, originally used for everything from bourbon to wine, and now the beers are expertly aged in them and sometimes blended by Meyers. In an era of American brewing when barrels are all the rage, Cambridge was way ahead of the curve and what winds up in your glass showcases that fact.

Not everything is hard and heavy. Cambridge also does session beers that are under 4 percent ABV, giving people a chance to enjoy several flavorful pints without regretting it the next day. Along with smaller glasses, pints, and pitchers, the brewery also serves towers, which are large clear cylinders of beer that come with their own tap handles, letting groups control their own pour.

That's why this Great American Beer Festival multi-medal-winning brewery continues to delight customers and leave them full but wanting more. Visit once and you'll be hooked.

Cambridge Brewing Company

Opened: 1989.
Owner: Phil Bannatyne.
Brewers: Will Meyers, brewmaster, and Jay Sullivan, lead brewer
System: 10-barrel Pub Brewing System.
Production: 2,000 barrels in 2011.
Hours: Daily, 11:30 A.M. to midnight.
Tours: By request.
Take-out beer: Growlers
Extras: Patio dining.

Special considerations: Handicapped-accessible.

Parking: Garage attached to complex.

Other area beers sites: See page 106.

John Harvard's Brewery & Ale House

33 Dunster Street, Cambridge, MA 02138
617-868-3585 • www.johnharvards.com

This is the original location of the once-mighty brewpub chain. Gary Gut and Grenville Byford, college friends who wanted to have their own English-style pub, opened here in 1992.

Harvard's was a great brewpub when it first opened. David Bertolini, who joined the company a few years after it started, said it was ahead of its time and more like the gastropubs we see today. Soon the chain began to grow with new locations in Framingham, Massachusetts (see page 65) and in the old Union Station Brewery in Providence, Rhode Island.

"Then it got geographically crazy," said Bertolini. An Atlanta location was opened just before the 1996 Olympic Games, then another one in Westport, Connecticut, followed by a Washington, D.C., location. Three opened in the Philadelphia area, one in the Pittsburgh area, and one in Wilmington, Delaware. Then came Cleveland, Long Island, and finally Manchester, Connecticut.

It was during this time that the company changed hands from its original owners to a venture capital firm and then to a company named Boston Culinary Group. Soon, locations began to close and by the time the current owners, Centerplate, took over, there were just four breweries left: the two Massachusetts locations, the one at Union Station in Rhode Island, and the one on Long Island.

During the time of expansion, the company wanted its locations to be streamlined and consistent, and so the menu was pared down to make it more simple, the beers were required to be brewed

Beers Brewed: John Harvard's Pale Ale, All American Light Lager, Nut Brown Ale, Dry Irish Stout, Old Willy India Pale Ale, Mid-Winter's Strong Ale, Celtic Red, Queen Bee Honey Beer, Wheat Beer, Summer Blonde, Oktoberfest, Holiday Red.

The Pick: There is a reason the Nut Brown Ale has won awards.

a certain way, and each location was required to have the same core beers on tap. Over the years the brand became, in a word, tired.

But the Connecticut-based Centerplate, which supplies food to entertainment venues like sports arenas and ski areas, is aiming to change all of that. "The beer brewing aspect of John Harvard's is something that is exciting," said Michael Kauffman, president of the Centerplate Restaurant Group. "It's one of those art forms that we are passionate about. We thought John Harvard's as a brand could be revived a bit."

This includes taking a look at revamping the menu, rethinking some beer recipes, and investing in new equipment. Indeed, the system at this location is so old that spare parts are either tough to come by or no longer exist.

As for the beers, Kauffman said, it will be up for the brewers to decide what is on tap. There will be some common beers, sure, but each location will have unique beers and brewers will be encouraged to share recipes.

The original John Harvard's has kept the English pub vibe with dark wood tables and copper accents. The lights are low and there are mercifully few televisions for distractions. There are a few stained glass windows depicting important historic figures and there's an ample dining room where groups can catch up over a meal. The servers are friendly and knowledgeable, and despite the old system, there is good beer being served.

There is still a loyal clientele for John Harvard's, and on nights and weekends it is routinely packed with undergrads and older folks, all enjoying mugs of beer and chatting about everything from world events to pop culture. It's a comfortable vibe, like a familiar friend's house that needs a fresh coat of paint and maybe some new furniture.

John Harvard's Brewery & Ale House

Opened: 1992.
Owner: Centerplate.
Brewers: Walker Modic and Jason Taggart.
System: 15-barrel Pub.
Production: 990 barrels in 2011.
Hours: Daily, 11:30 A.M. to 1 A.M.
Tours: Saturdays, 2 P.M. to 4 P.M.
Take-out beer: Growlers.
Special considerations: Handicapped-accessible.
Parking: On street. The brewery validates for specific garages in area.
Other area beer sites: See page 106.

Deadwood Café & Brewery

820 Morrissey Boulevard, Boston, MA 02122
617-825-3800 • www.deadwoodbrewery.com

Located inside an entertainment complex known as Boston Bowl, the Deadwood Café & Brewery is an admirable attempt for a corporate owner, in this case the Phillips Family Hospitality company, to embrace the growing craft beer scene.

The brewery opened in 2009, but Boston Bowl has been around since 1959 and enjoys the kind of reputation that is earned over decades of operation. Matt Sammartino helms the brewery and said when it came time to look at ways to revive Boston Bowl, he looked to a hobby that he and his father had been enjoying: homebrewing.

Now with a space that fits in nicely around the lanes, Matt can brew and serve up pilsners, hefeweizens, and IPAs to those looking for a sip between rolls and something to celebrate that score of 300. Education plays a big role in moving the house beers. They still keep some of the bigger brands behind the bar, but servers are encouraged to offer samples of house beers. Matt said that when league season starts, newcomers will usually stick with a familiar commercial brew, but nine out of ten will convert to the house-made beers by the time the season ends. "We sell a lot of pitchers," he told us.

The pilsner is the most popular, but Matt holds a fondness for hoppier offerings and has been slowly converting people to his IPA, which is the number two seller these days.

Bowling and beer mix well together. But sometimes you want to break away from the crashing pins and cheering teams and just relax quietly with a glass of beer. There are two hotels on the Boston Bowl property, also owned by Phillips Family Hospitality, and growlers are offered on the room service menu. That's right, along with a club sandwich or pasta dish you can get a cold, freshly poured growler of beer that was made just steps from your room door.

Come for the bowling, stay for the beer, and if you're too tired to leave, just get a room. Deadwood has you covered.

Beers Brewed: Pilsner, Nut Brown, IPA, Red Ale, Bock Dark, and seasonal offerings.

The Pick: The Red Ale blends English brewing sensibilities with the hop kick of the Pacific Northwest.

Deadwood Café & Brewery

Opened: 2009.

Owners: Phil Strazzula and Joe Sammartino.

Brewers: Matt Sammartino and Jack Torchetti.

System: Four stainless steel 155-gallon brew kettles and fermenters.

Production: 210 barrels in 2011.

Hours: Monday through Thursday, 11 A.M. to 1 A.M.; Friday and Sunday, 10 A.M to 2 A.M.

Tours: By appointment.

Take-out beer: 64-ounce growlers.

Extras: Boston Bowl is open 24 hours, with 30 tenpin lanes, 14 candlepin lanes, 12 pool tables, batting cages, and more than 80 interactive video games. Brewery store with Deadwood merchandise, including pint glasses, growlers, blankets, and T-shirts.

Special considerations: Handicapped-accessible.

Parking: Free parking and a courtesy shuttle to and from the local JFK subway stop.

Other area beer sites: See page 106.

Watch City Brewing Company

256 Moody Street, Waltham, MA 02453
(781) 647-4000 • www.watchcitybrew.com

For those who lament the disappearance of Main Street and loathe strip malls and the seemingly anonymous employees working at cookie-cutter box stores, there is hope in Waltham.

There is actually a Main Street in this suburb west of Boston along the commuter rail line. We found ourselves strolling up and down Moody Street, where Indian and Italian restaurants mix with locally owned bookshops and bodegas and barbers take up storefronts. And there on the corner of Pine Street is the Watch City Brewing Company.

Identifiable by the clock outside and a white neon sign, this staple in the Massachusetts brewing scene has been around since 1996, pouring its creative pints to a public that cannot seem to get enough. That is largely thanks to Aaron Mateychuk, the brewer who admires Sam Calagione, founder and brewer at Delaware's Dogfish Head Craft Ales, a man who is not afraid to bend the rationale of beer.

Mateychuk had not yet arrived during one of our more recent visits, but Carol was bartending. Spend enough time at Watch City and you will know who is bartending just by the music playing over the satellite radio. Classic Vinyl was on, meaning Carol was the one pouring pints. She set up samples at the bar, everything from the golden ale to the imperial IPA. From the beer engine she produced a cask ale made with bacon and rosemary. The botanical aroma was overwhelming and stuck around through the first taste and finish, but showed the inventiveness of Mateychuk.

When he did arrive and was asked about the ale, he took on an impish grin. He created nearly twenty variations on the cask, he explained, and this was the last one. It was achieved by a "super secret" method using alcohol to wash the 60 pounds of bacon used to concoct the ale. He was already thinking about the next round. Mateychuk also grows about 90 percent of the botanicals he uses in the house beers.

Beers Brewed: Moody Street Stout, Tick Tock Golden Ale, Titan Ale, Shillelagh Irish Red Nitro Ale, Hops Explosion IPA, MonkeyMonk Saison, Stephanie's Cherry Raspberry Wit, Lunarshine Burleywhine, Clockwork Summer Ale, 'FNA Imperial IPA.

The Pick: Find out what Aaron has on cask, and it is likely your best bet. Find out what real ale is all about and enjoy an ale right from the handpull.

"After eighteen years of brewing these are the beers I want to make," said Mateychuk. "You get to a point where you've copied and followed examples and now it's time to make great beers that don't follow any styles."

He spends time thinking about where beer came from, what brewers from centuries ago had to contend with, and what ingredients they had available. He then applies it to his own recipes.

The brewing system is visible from the street. It's traditional equipment with some aesthetic enhancements, like wood paneling on the mash tun and brick covering on the kettle. The fermentation vessels and conditioning tanks are in the basement in chilled rooms that were built around them when the brewery was installed. Getting anything in or out that is larger than, say, a few kegs will require a great deal of construction and work.

We were at the bar, a satisfying long slate affair with fixed wooden stools like you'd see at a diner, and Mateychuk brought out a saison he was currently working on. One taste, even before carbonation, and it was easy to see why customers keep coming back.

The food doesn't hurt either. The menu is decidedly pub fare— sandwiches, burgers, chili, and a fish and chips platter the size of your head. One heart-stopping item stands out: the Tick Tock Beer Battered Burger, described on the menu as "dipped in Watch City's own beer batter recipe and deep fried. Topped with chipotle-lime mayo." That's right. A deep-fried burger. It's glorious.

It's not just the beers and menu that make Watch City a destination. It's the overall feel of the place. Artwork from a nearby community is selected by owner Jocelyn McLaughlin and displayed on the wall as available for sale. It adds some color to the walls but also highlights the commitment the brewpub has to the community and local businesses.

This commitment is also highlighted by the relationship Watch City has with the Landmark Embassy Theater, located just next door. Come in for dinner before a movie and someone from the restaurant will actually go next door and pick up tickets, at a discounted rate, and bring them back to your table. After the show, bring your stub back in and you get a discount on a nightcap. It just adds to the overall Main Street feel of this local tavern and its commitment to not only customers but also fellow businesses.

It would also seem like low-hanging fruit to round out this profile with clock references, ticking off various clichés about time. Waltham is known as Watch City, thanks to its history. The Waltham Watch Company was one of the world's premier precision-instrument makers from its founding in the late 1800s to 1957. Its factory complex, the first to make watches on an assembly line, is now a historic district. It remains a point of pride for Waltham, but the brewery really does not play up the watch thing. In fact, the only clock to be found in the brewpub is in the brewhouse itself, there to inform Mateychuk when it's time to move on to the next step.

Before hitting the road, Mateychuk had one more beer to pour: his super malty but very smooth barley wine named Lunarshine Burleywhine. It was on cask that day and aged for three months in Jim Beam bourbon barrels. There was certainly time for one more beer, in that case—and there was no better way to end the day.

Watch City Brewing Company

Opened: 1996.

Owner: Jocelyn McLaughlin.

Brewers: Aaron Mateychuk, head brewer and Kelly McKnight, assistant brewer.

System: 14-barrel Pugsley direct-fire kettle

Production: 619 barrels in 2011.

Hours: Monday through Saturday, 11:30 A.M. to 12:30 A.M.; Sunday 11:30 A.M to 11:30 P.M.

Tours: By appointment.

Take-out beer: Growlers and 22-ounce bottles.

Extras: Occasional live music. Beer events.

Special considerations: Handicapped-accessible.

Parking: Two-floor garage in rear lot.

Other area beer sites: See page 106.

Idle Hands Craft Ales

3 Charlton Street, Unit 4, Everett, MA 02149
617-819-4263 • www.idlehandscraftales.com

The devil finds work for idle hands, the saying goes. But there is nothing sinister about the area's newest nanobrewery. In fact, with a positive outlook, commitment to the locavore movement, and a welcoming attitude to visitors at their industrial-space brewery, things are downright heavenly for Christopher and Grace Tkach, a husband and wife team who opened their doors in late 2011.

Both spouses have backgrounds in business, but Chris was less than happy in his day job, so when talking about the future, as newlywed couples do, a plan was hatched to open a brewery. Chris had been homebrewing for years and had developed a passion for Belgian-style ales. In looking at the breweries in the Boston area, they realized that they could fill the Belgian niche and got to work securing space, going through the licensing process, and preparing to open their doors to the public.

But, first they had to clear the state Alcohol Beverage Control Commission. Idle Hands had applied for a farmer-brewery license, not unlike many others in the state. But the agency responded with revised rules requiring breweries with the license to "grow at least 50 percent, in the aggregate, of the quantity of cereal grains and hops needed to produce the anticipated volume of malt beverages."

Beers Brewed: Pandora, Patriarch, Cognition, Triplication.

Given their location, that would be difficult. The same is true for the other breweries in the state (Boston Beer Company and Harpoon both have one). Lack of that particular license would mean a

The Pick: Pandora. This 6-percent Belgian Pale Ale has delightful spice and citrus notes, resulting in a refreshing libation.

halt to on-site tastings and self-distribution. The issue was resolved long enough for Idle Hands to start dispensing beer and to keep the other places open.

Idle Hands is decidedly a nanobrewery, eking out 1.5 barrels at a time. And they have secured contracts with a number of restaurants who focus on local cuisine and creative dishes. The addition of a local beer is sure to elevate the overall meal.

Their flagship beer is a Belgian-style pale ale called Pandora. For now this is the beer that will be most readily available. They are also producing a Belgian single called Patriarch, which will be brewed with each new yeast batch, said Christopher, and there is a plan for a wit named Brevity to join the ranks at some point.

With a lot of buzz around their opening and the daily pressures of running a business, the couple is constantly busy, never idle. But, they are always up for visitors at the brewery.

Idle Hands Craft Ales

Opened: 2011.

Owners: Christopher and Grace Tkach.

Brewer: Christopher Tkach.

System: Self-designed 1$1/2$-barrel system.

Production: 7$1/2$ barrels in 2011.

Tours: By appointment

Take-out beer: Growlers.

Extras: Happy hours. Live music. Idle Hands merchandise for sale, including T-shirts and tap handles.

Parking: Street parking

Other area beer site: See page 106.

Trillium Brewing Company

369 Congress Street, Boston, MA 02120
617-453-8745 • www.trilliumbrewing.com

The trillium is a flower native to North America that can take up to seven years to bear its first bloom. This is a frustratingly long time for people who appreciate beauty and good things. After spending two years trying to get his brewery off the ground, Jean-Claude Tetreault was beginning to empathize with the flower.

The intention for Trillium—slated for a fall 2012 opening in Boston's Fort Point neighborhood—is to be an American farmhouse brewery. "We're going to use lots of local ingredients and look at the Belgian and French farmhouse styles for inspiration," Tetreault told us. This will mean some wild-fermented beers, barrel aging, and using locally grown grains and hops. He looks to existing American breweries like Michigan's Jolly Pumpkin Artisan Ales for inspiration and will be filling a niche in the increasingly crowded metro beer market.

With their ten-barrel brewhouse, Tetreault wants to create what he calls "New American craft," which relies more on the artisinal process and using unconventional ingredients on traditional styles. This includes a pale ale brewed with oats or a hoppy red ale with some unmalted rye. "This is what I feel like American craft brewing would have evolved to sooner if there were not culture bombs like Prohibition, then industrialization, and, ultimately commoditization of beer and the wipeout that happened from that," he said.

We weren't able to sample any of the beers before publication, but if Tetreault's enthusiasm matches his recipes, best to get in line at the brewery now.

Trillium Brewing Company

Opened: 2012.
Owners: Jean-Claude and Esther Tetreault.
Brewer: Jean-Claude Tetreault.
System: Custom-fabricated Practical Fusion 10-barrel direct-fired brewhouse.
Production: N/A
Tours: Not available.

Take-out beer: Growlers and bottles.

Special considerations: Handicapped-accessible.

Parking: Limited metered street parking and nearby parking garages.

Other area beer sites: See page 106.

Night Shift Brewing

3 Charlton Street, Everett, MA 02149
978-270-6613 • www.nightshiftbrewing.com

Seeing as they all had day jobs, the three founders of Night Shift usually found themselves getting batches in when they could. More often than not they wound up working the third shift. Of course that was when they were just homebrewers, long before they started their own production brewery. As one of the founders, Michael Oxton, explains, "it just wasn't possible to do it at any other time."

Now that they have their own digs, however, don't expect the schedule to change too much. As one of the state's newest breweries, they have an ambitious plan to get kegs and 22-ounce bottles to restaurants and package stores and to make sure there is enough supply to meet their expected demand.

That means constantly brewing on their 3^1/2-barrel system, including after hours. Take a close look at their logo and you'll see it's a hop cone fashioned to look like an owl. A nice subtle touch in our opinion.

Oxton met friend and co-owner Robert Burns when the two were undergrads at Maine's Bowdoin College. The third partner, Michael O'Mara, was a childhood friend of Rob's. Oxton and Burns got into homebrewing while in college and continued the hobby after moving to Boston. O'Mara was living in Philadelphia but the three got together for collaboration beers and soon realized that they had something special on their hands. They spent the next year forming a company, putting together a business plan, and securing invest-

Beers Brewed: Trifecta, Bee Tea, Taza Stout, Quad Reserve, Somer Weisse, Viva Habanera.

The Pick: Somer Weisse. This tart and flavorful Berliner Weisse is a different take on a warm-weather offering. Seek it out and enjoy.

ments. All this happened on the side while the trio continued toiling away at their day jobs.

At night they played with and perfected recipes, getting the beers to where they wanted them to be commercially. They are following the Dogfish Head model, using off-centered ingredients with classic recipes. So there is an India pale ale brewed with a Belgian yeast strain and mangos and a stout brewed with cocoa nibs. "We'll use strange, random ingredients," Oxton told us. "That is what will make our brewery interesting. We are staying untraditional and unorthodox."

Their location, inside a warehouse in this Boston suburb, houses another brewing company, Idle Hands, another new brewer to the scene. Oxton and partners had heard there was space available in Everett and when they arrived to check it out, Chris from Idle Hands was there. Seeing how the two breweries are going in different directions, it will likely be a friendly relationship and not a Hatfields and McCoys situation. In fact, to save money the breweries are collaborating on shipments of ingredients, said Oxton.

"We're not competitive," he told us. In fact, both breweries are hoping that visitors will take time to visit both places, an easy proposition since they share a physical wall. However, for now there are no plans for nocturnal visiting hours. So it's best to arrive when the sun is still up.

Night Shift Brewing

Opened: 2012.

Owners: Michael Oxton, Michael O'Mara, and Robert Burns.

Brewers: Michael Oxton, Michael O'Mara, and Robert Burns.

System: Psycho Brew System.

Production: N/A

Tours: By appointment.

Take-out beer: Growlers, specialty bottles.

Extras: Beer tastings. Music studio with frequent live sessions. Merchandise store, with glassware, hats, and T-shirts.

Special considerations: Handicapped-accessible.

Parking: Lots in front and rear, lots of spaces

Other area beer sites: See page 106.

Blue Hills Brewery

1020 Turnpike St. #3B, Canton, MA 02021
781-821-2337 • www.bluehillsbrewery.com

Andris Veidis says it was his lifelong dream to work in a brewery of his own. For a long while he was living that dream, in part, but it was under the vision of others. He first started out as a brewer for a number of different companies and then later worked installing brewing systems around the country for upstart craft breweries, run by people already capitalizing on their own entrepreneurial dreams. It was fun and rewarding work, he said, and during that time he was able to learn about an important side of the business.

So when it came time to put his own business plan together, he was more educated than most. And after it was approved and he was licensed, installing the equipment was, well, easy. So easy, in fact, that Veidis was able to open within nine months of getting his business plan in order—no small feat (ask just about any other brewery). Blue Hills Brewery brewed its first batch on New Year's Eve 2008 and has been running strong ever since.

Veidis and business partner Peter Augis, who runs the sales and promotional side of things, looked around for a while before settling down in Canton. They wanted to be close to Boston but also in a small community they could serve. "We're nothing without our community," Veidis told us. "Part of our mission statement is 'community oriented, community wide.'"

Drive past too quickly and you'll miss the brewery. It's smack in the middle of an aging strip mall in the South Shore area and largely unremarkable from the outside. However, cross through the threshold and you're greeted by a comfortable taproom and office. Here, samples are poured from behind a six-foot pilsner-shaped pint glass. When we arrived early one morning, Augis was busy waxing it, giving it a perfect shine that would soon be marred by spilled samples and condensation rings. "This is a daily ritual," he said.

Beers Brewed: Dunkelweizen, India Pale Ale, Imperial Red I.P.A., Black Hops, Antimatter, OktoBrau, Wampatuck Wheat, Watermelon Wheat.

The Pick: Antimatter is a rotating series from Blue Hills that uses just one kind of malt and one hop variety. The results have been pleasing and surprising. By focusing on just one ingredient, the beer allows it to shine brighter and show off its true characteristics.

Augis has been a salesman his whole life and now says he has the chance to ply what he really enjoys—good beer. Like others in the industry, he's out at all hours, going from bar to bar talking up his beer, signing new accounts and problem-solving for owners and managers. He's a passionate fellow with a great appreciation of history, pride in his Latvian heritage, and a lot of ideas he would like to see come to life.

He told us that Canton played one of the key roles in the American Revolution. There was once a mansion, just up the road from where the brewery stands today, where patriots gathered to hold the very first meeting in the colony of Massachusetts to discuss opposition to the tyranny of Great Britain.

As Augis was launching into all the ideas that the brewery can do to keep this historical memory alive, Veidis entered and the conversation turned to the line of beers Blue Hills is producing. "We design the beers to be unique amongst each other," he said. There are twists on old styles, such as the Black Hops Ale or Imperial Red IPA. In the summer they release a watermelon beer that is tough to keep stocked on shelves. Their preferred method of packaging is 22-ounce bottles, but growler fills are available from the taproom.

The brewery is a glorious mishmash of equipment wedged into corners and tight spaces, making the most out of what room they have. Veidis and Augis have worked some creative innovations into the building to solve some problems like condensation, draining, and energy use.

It's a fun brewery to visit and seems like a fun place to work as well. Veidis told us he lets the brewery interns get together and brew their own recipes—exercises that have yielded delicious results, like an excellent milk stout.

Veidis keeps coming around to the community theme. He is earnest when he expresses thanks to all those who helped him realize this dream. "There was a lot of family and a lot of friends, a lot of people who got us here," he told us. "They believed in this brewery and we've been rolling ever since."

And about the name: The Blue Hills were so called by early settlers who noticed a bluish hue coming from the slopes as they sailed the coastline. It's an area worth exploring and soaking in, reminding yourself that you're not very far from a thriving metropolis. And when you return from all that nature, there are pints waiting just down the road.

Blue Hills Brewery

Opened: 2009.

Owners: Andris Veidis, Peter Augis, Martin Grots, Talis Veidis, and Mik Veidis.

Brewer: Andris Veidis.

System: 20-barrel Pub Steam Brewhouse

Production: 2,200 barrels in 2011.

Hours: Wednesday, 5 P.M. to 8 P.M.; Friday, 3:30 P.M. to 6:30 P.M.; Saturday, 2 P.M. to 6 P.M.

Tours: Friday, 3:30 P.M. to 6:30 P.M., and Saturday, 2 P.M. to 6 P.M.

Take-out beer: Six-packs, bombers, growlers, kegs.

Special considerations: Handicapped-accessible.

Parking: Plenty available.

Other area beer sites:

- **Four Square Restaurant and Bar** (16 Commercial Street, Braintree, 781-848-4448, www.foursquarebar.com)
- **Fat Cat** (24 Chestnut Street, Quincy, 617-471-4363, www.fatcatrestaurant.com)
- **Union Brew House** (550 Washington Street, Weymouth, 781-340-0440, www.unionbrewhouse.com)

Rhode Island Breweries
by Chris O'Leary

The Rhode Island beer scene has seen its ups and downs. During the early 1980s, a low point in our nation's modern brewing history, my hometown of Cranston lost its precious Narragansett Brewery, and the region lost a heritage brand. I remember driving by the big red-and-white brick hull of the brewery, with its iconic red-and-gold seal, as it was finally demolished in 1998. Bit by bit, the memory of the brand faded into oblivion. At the same time, one West Warwick–based brewery, Emerald Isle, and two Rhode Island–based beer marketing companies who contracted out their brewing, Great Providence and Hope Brewing, had recently failed. For a state that once saw more than one million barrels of annual production out of just one brewery, tearing down the Gansett Brewery was a reminder of how far we'd fallen.

But even at that time, some successful small brewers were picking up the brewing tradition where 'Gansett left off. Trinity Brewhouse, Coddington Brewing, and Union Station Brewery were already mild successes in bringing new, flavorful ales to Rhode Islanders. Coastal Extreme Brewing, the first place where beer had been bottled in Rhode Island since Narragansett's closing, opened six months later. We were on the right track.

And then, the stagnation. Rhode Island has been notorious for having a bad climate for small business, and smaller brewers refrained from taking the risk to open here, even though the influence we get from nearby Massachusetts has boosted demand for craft beer in the Ocean State. Today, there are five breweries in Rhode Island. That's the same number that operated after the repeal of Prohibition. That's the same number that existed in 2000. Maybe there's something to this whole stagnation thing.

But there's hope. We have some bright minds in brewing, like Sean Larkin and Derek Luke, who have vastly improved their products and have embraced collaboration among Rhode Island's small group of brewers. We have new breweries, like Larkin's Revival and the forthcoming Grey Sail in Westerly. We have the remarkable rebirth of Narragansett Brewing, with founder Mark Hellendrung, who's aggressively pushing for a brewery to be built in this state.

But most importantly, we have a unique identity. Rhode Islanders are very protective and very proud of their state's name and heritage, and are increasingly supporting local agriculture and business to turn the tide in the midst of the worst business downturn in the state's recent history. This, by a stroke of luck, coincides with larger out-of-state brewers pulling out of Rhode Island in recent years. Maybe now there's more room on store shelves and bar taps for local beer and a better chance for Rhode Islanders to support their local craft brewery.

- **Coastal Extreme Brewing Company** (293 JT Connell Road, Newport, RI 02840, 401-849-5232, www.newportstorm.com). Also home to the Thomas Tew Distillery, this production brewery releases an ambitious line of regular, seasonal, and specialty beers. Founded by four college friends, Coastal Extreme has been around since 1999 and has amassed a strong following.

- **Coddington Brewing Company** (210 Coddington Highway, Middletown, RI 02842, 401-847-6690, www.newport-brewery.com). This brewpub has been serving up pints since 1995. Named after the founder of Newport, Rhode Island, the brewery produces a large selection of beers, making sure that each time you visit, you'll find something new on tap.

- **Grey Sail Brewing Company LLC** (63 Canal Street, Westerly, RI 02891, 410-212-7592, www.greysailbrewing.com). Run by a husband and wife team, this is one of the state's newest breweries, having opened in late 2011.

- **Mohegan Cafe and Brewery** (213 Water Street, Block Island, RI 02807, 401-466-5911). The only brewery on this popular vacation island, the house brews are popular with tourists and locals. There are usually about five on tap at any given time.

- **Trinity Brewhouse** (186 Fountain Street, Providence, RI 02903, 401-453-2337, www.trinitybrewhouse.com). This popular downtown brewpub is a magnet for good times by customers who appreciate good food and great beer. The latter is thanks to brewmaster Sean Larkin, who has perfected the beers that constantly flow from the taps.

Coastal Massachusetts

What better way to leave behind the bustle of the city than to head towards the sea? From Boston, you have plenty of choices for a day at the beach, but the first one you make is the most important—to head south or north. There are a lot of vital differences, so choose carefully.

We'll start here with the area called South of Boston, particularly the South Shore, which is a mix of beautiful coastal towns, wide-open beaches, small islands, and larger cities. This is Bristol County, sandwiched between Rhode Island and Cape Cod, roughly one hour south of Boston. This part of the state has a strong maritime history, with scattered charming seaside towns, but also a strong industrial heritage.

Most famous by far is Plymouth, of course, although you'd have to live under a rock not to know this story. Plymouth is where the Pilgrims set up the first permanent settlement in New England. They established Plymouth Colony in 1620, naming the town after the *Mayflower*'s port in England. After a long and tormenting transatlantic voyage, the Pilgrims sought refuge in this protected bay area and put down roots alongside the local Wampanoag Native Americans, who'd been living off the land in this region for many thousands of years. This is where the famous first Thanksgiving was celebrated, with the 53 surviving Pilgrims (out of an original 102) sharing a meal alongside Squanto, a Pawtuxet tribe member associated with the Wampanoags. Squanto, in a rare moment of accord between the two cultures, taught the Pilgrims how to harvest the land and brokered alliances among the Pilgrims and the Wampanoags to live peacefully alongside each other.

Although the Pilgrims were the first English immigrants to settle here permanently, they were almost immediately followed by other British explorers and travelers, who soon after arriving set up thriving fishing and trading posts in areas that later would become cities. The entire area has been excellently preserved by local conservationist groups, and traveling through here today you can see a lot of the natural beauty and resources that the settlers would have experienced, and even some of the original Pilgrim homes.

Other nearby communities are New Bedford, which was briefly settled in 1602, well before nearby Plymouth, but as the settlers soon retreated to their native England, all of the fame landed on Plymouth. But New Bedford eventually became a major player on the whaling scene, and for the second half of the nineteenth century was considered to be a more important whaling center than even nearby Nantucket. When the whaling industry declined after the discovery of petroleum in 1859, New Bedford relied on its other industries, mainly manufacturing and fishing, and remained a thriving city. That history paved the way for the future, and it's now a bustling city of more than 100,000 people, with a distinct Portuguese influence evidenced by its great and authentic restaurants and local festivals.

If what you want is to get away from it all, you can't do better than Cuttyhunk Island, a two-mile-long island about twelve miles south of New Bedford and eight miles west of Martha's Vineyard. Accessible by ferry from New Bedford, Cuttyhunk has only the barest smattering of restaurants and local businesses, but is known for its unblemished natural beauty. Golf carts are the preferred method of transportation, but you can also grab a bicycle or just use your feet. Keep in mind there are virtually no ATMs on the island and very few businesses take credit cards, so plan your cash flow accordingly before you arrive.

If you've decided to head north instead, your options are many. Although the North Shore is smaller than the South Shore geographically speaking, with just thirty miles of coastline, this area north of Boston feels arguably more connected to the ocean somehow. The coastline is rocky and occasionally severe, but gorgeous. This is Essex County, made up of thirty-four towns and cities, and full of hidden beaches, bustling harbors, cozy hotels, and country inns. Here, a sense of industry—the industry of the sea—prevails, with a major emphasis on fishing, yachting, whale-watching, and of course, tourism.

The entire North of Boston area was actually named after a book of poetry by Robert Frost, published in 1914 under the same name. Frost was raised in Lawrence, Massachusetts, and in his lifetime won four Pulitzer Prizes for his work. The Robert Frost Festival (www.frost

foundation.org) is held in his honor every October, with walking tours of sites that were important in his life and work.

One great place to get a true North Shore vibe is Marblehead, located a meager seventeen miles north of Boston. Known as the "Yachting Capital of the World," Marblehead is full of fabulous old-money mansions worthy of a gawk or two, but also has quaint, narrow streets lined with old colonial homes, shopping boutiques, elegant restaurants, and stunning harbor views.

Also surprisingly close to Boston is Salem, home of the world-famous witch trials of the late seventeenth century. The atmosphere in Salem is thick with spookiness, even on a sunshine-filled late August afternoon such as when we were in town. You can instantly understand why this town has a reputation as the best place to be on Halloween and why it's so popular with tourists year-round. It's beautiful, pitch-perfect at capitalizing off its gothic history while still retaining the charm of a simple village against the sea.

As you continue north you'll hit Cape Ann, a rocky outcropping out into the Atlantic known as "Massachusetts' Other Cape," home to the city of Gloucester, as well as the smaller towns of Rockport, Essex, and Manchester-by-the-Sea. This entire region is stunning, with its granite cliffs and sandy shorelines, and feels a little more like Maine than nearby Cape Cod.

Gloucester, despite its claim to fame as the setting of the 2000 movie *The Perfect Storm*, is less for tourists and more of a traditional fishing village, with a bustling harbor, a smattering of salty old restaurants and bars clinging to the water's edge, and scattered community beaches along the bay. While you're in town, walk along the waterfront to see the famous Man at the Wheel statue, also known as the Gloucester Fisherman's Memorial (www.nps.gov/nr/travel/maritime/glo.htm). Finished in 1925, this larger-than-life bronze statue of a fisherman clutching the wheel of a ship, fighting his way through stormy seas while clad in soaked-through oilskins, is haunting. The inscription reads "They That Go Down To The Sea In Ships 1623–1923" in honor of the more than ten thousand local fishermen, a staggering number, who perished at sea during Gloucester's first three hundred years. The statue looks out over the harbor and a constant stream of visitors flows through to admire it and take in the views.

Nearby and far more touristy is Rockport, an old fishing village turned artists' community, popular with photographers, painters, and sculptors. If you're passing through the small town of Essex for lunch, make sure to get the local specialty—fried clams. This is the birthplace of the dish, and it can't be missed. Or stop by the village of Manchester-by-the-Sea for a dip in the ocean at the Singing Beach, the most popular North Shore beach (because it's connected to Boston by public transportation).

As you head north from Cape Ann towards the New Hampshire border, you'll hit a few more gems: Newburyport and Ipswich. Newburyport is a perfect waterfront city with a pedestrian-friendly brick downtown and wonderful views. Ipswich is famous for Crane Beach, an extremely popular swimming spot, and for its dozens of perfectly preserved seventeenth-century houses.

No matter what your style is, you can't beat coastal Massachusetts in terms of gorgeous ocean, the freshest seafood imaginable, and oceans that are so cold you'll go completely numb but be invigorated after taking a dip.

Here are some recommendations for lodging as you travel the coast.

- **The Bradford Inn & Suites** (www.governorbradford.com), in Plymouth, is a popular favorite in South Shore territory. It overlooks Plymouth Harbor and is within walking distance of downtown restaurants and shopping.

- **White Swan Bed and Breakfast** (www.whiteswan.com) is the location in Plymouth for something a little more intimate. The two-hundred-year-old farmhouse turned bed-and-breakfast is just a two-minute walk from the beach, where bike and kayak rentals are available.

- **The Cuttyhunk Fishing Club** (www.cuttyhunkfishingclub-bb.com), in Cuttyhunk, is a family-owned bed-and-breakfast set on eight acres overlooking the sea. It's perfect for quiet time, but is only open from mid-May through early October.

- **Cape Ann Motor Inn** (http://capeannmotorinn.com), in Gloucester, is perfect if you're looking for convenience. It's one of the only beachfront hotels in town, with beautiful views and great family amenities.

- **The Salem Inn** (www.saleminnma.com), in Salem, is made up of three different historic homes, all refurbished to combine a sense of history with modern-day comforts. It's within walking distance to all local attractions and has an inviting continental breakfast included in its rates.

Here is a sampling of attractions and activities in the region that will surely enhance your visits to the brewery.

- **Plymouth Rock** (www.visit-plymouth.com/plymouthrock.htm) is an American icon that is a necessary stop.

- **Plimoth Plantation** (www.visit-plymouth.com/plimothplantation
.htm) is a Smithsonian-affiliated living history museum that showcases life in a seventeenth-century colonial village, juxtaposed
against life in a traditional Native American camp.

- **New Bedford Whaling Museum** (www.whalingmuseum.org), in
New Bedford, has more than 150,000 whaling artifacts and the
world's largest ship model.

- **Battleship Cove** (www.battleshipcove.org), in Fall River, is the
home port for the World War II battleship USS *Massachusetts* and a
one-ton model of the *Titanic*.

- **Edaville USA** (www.edaville.com), in Carver, is an antique-style
amusement park with a two-mile-long narrow-gauge railroad and
vintage amusement park rides.

- **Cranberry Harvest Festival** (www.cranberries.org/festival/festi
val.html) is held annually the second weekend in October and is a
great way to get into the spirit of cranberry country, with food
vendors, musical performances, children's activities, and more.
More than 12,000 acres of cranberry bogs are in Massachusetts,
with more than 450 growers producing crops. Harvests are in September and October.

- **Salem Witch Museum** (www.salemwitchmuseum.com), in Salem,
offers a bit of local history about the hysteria of the 1692 witch
trials held here.

- **Salem Maritime National Historic Site** (www.nps.gov/sama) is a
nine-acre park that celebrates Salem's past as the most important
port in the United States.

- **Cape Ann Whale Watch** (www.seethewhales.com) has regular
departures from Gloucester. If you're more interested in wildlife,
you can't do better than whale-watching. Massachusetts is one of
the top whale-watching spots in the world, with charters running
from April through October.

Just Beer

just beer:
american grown ales

98 Horseneck Road, Westport, MA 02790
www.justbeer.us

Bill Russell thinks of it as the band that records a great album, goes on the road for a stretch, performs the same material night after night after night, and eventually starts feeling like their sound is tired. So, they get off the road, go back into the studio, and reinvent themselves.

That's how Russell, the head honcho at Just Beer, described the decision to change the name and focus of his original brewery, Buzzard's Bay. That brewery, founded in 1998, focused on English-style ales, using all English ingredients. When they opened it was a way to differentiate themselves from other breweries in the area and it allowed them to grow. In fact, Buzzard Bay beers were available in stores from Virginia to Maine.

But inside the brewery was "a lot of tension," Russell told us. Having a brewery located on a community-minded farm, the thought was to retune their focus and pay more attention to the area around them. So, they pulled the plug on Buzzard's Bay in 2009, changed their name to Just Beer, and dramatically scaled back production. That's right. In a day and age where small breweries are fighting tooth and nail to grow their market share, Russell and his team went the other way. "For all that Buzzard's Bay was, we lost our way," he explained. "We originally launched and were creative and enjoyed the making of beer, but that got tired."

Now, they are distributed in five or so surrounding communities full of "a lot of dedicated beer drinkers" and are using only American-grown ingredients. "American farmers are more important to support than English farmers, or German or Czech farmers," Russell said.

While they are not growing their own hops (yet) or grain, the brewery is on a farm of more than five hundred acres that is also home to a vineyard and winery named Westport Rivers. They also raise cattle for beef, grow hay for the local dairy community, and have a vegetable garden. With that extra space the brewery had, they began to contract brew for some local breweries, like Pretty Things, Offshore Ales, and Blatant Brewery. "All the brewers from those places are terrific and really hands on," said Russell.

Beers Brewed: The Golden Flounder, Semper Fi PA, MobyD, and rotating and seasonal beers.

The Pick: The Golden Flounder is a pale ale that gets the job done.

The brews that Just Beer now focuses on tend towards the American experimental and "goofy," said Russell, and the local customers are enjoying their locally crafted pints. The brewers are having more fun as well, according to Russell: "It's about progress, not perfection, and we're enjoying the creative process."

Just Beer

Opened: 2009 (Buzzard's Bay, 1998).

Owners: Russell family.

Brewers: Harry Smith and Bill Russell.

System: 50-barrel Newlands.

Production: 1,000 barrels of Just Beer and 3,500 barrels for custom clients in 2011.

Hours: Saturday, 11 P.M. to 5 P.M.

Tours: Saturday, 11 P.M. to 5 P.M.

Take-out beer: Bottles and growlers.

Special considerations: Handicapped-accessible.

Parking: On site.

Other area beer sites: The following bars all serve Just Beer and are worth a visit.

- **The Pour Farm Tavern** (780 Purchase Street, New Bedford, 508-990-1123, www.pourfarm.com).
- **Rose Alley** (94 Front Street, New Bedford, 508-858-5123, www.drinkrose alley.com).
- **South Coast Local** (81 Fairhaven Road, Mattapoisett, 508-758-3600, www. thesouthlocal.com).
- **Bittersweet Tavern** (438 Main Road, Westport, 508-636-0085).

Mayflower Brewing Company

12 Resnik Road, Plymouth, MA 02360
508-746-2674 • www.mayflowerbrewing.com

Drew Brosseau was just a teenager when the country's first modern microbrewery—the one that would launch a revolution—opened in his hometown of Sonoma, California. Working inside an old building and using repurposed and self-made equipment, Jack McAuliffe opened

New Albion Brewing in the mid-1970s. That extraordinary act more than thirty years ago led the revolution that would become American craft beer.

Not that it's ordinary for people to open breweries; it's just more common now than it was in McAuliffe's day. And one of those breweries is Mayflower, where Brosseau is founder and president.

For him, this is a second career, but one that seems like he was destined to pursue. He has ties to the very first brewers who set foot on the shores of a new country. The Pilgrims landed in Plymouth in 1620 after sixty-five days at sea. "We could not now take time for further search or consideration, our victuals being much spent, especially our beer," wrote William Bradford, one of the passengers onboard.

One passenger on that historic ship was John Alden, who earned his living as a cooper of beer barrels. Ten generations later, his descendent, Drew Brosseau, would open a brewery of his own not far from where his ancestor started a new life.

When Brosseau retired from the technology and banking industry in the mid-1990s the idea to open his own brewery began rattling around in his head again. Having married a woman from Massachusetts, he knew there would be no returning to California, but Plymouth was an attractive destination. No one had yet claimed the Mayflower name and, given his family history, everything seemed to fit just right.

It wasn't until 2007 that the brewery opened and since then Brosseau and his team have worked to create flavorful ales with an English bent. "I've watched the industry develop over the years and there are breweries that are abandoning traditional styles," he told us. "I wanted to brew traditional ales that taste great. We also don't have fancy names. Our porter is a porter, our pale ale is just that. No zany names for us."

From the start business has been good. He is focused on the southeastern part of the state and has seen double-digit growth over the years. "We are selling all we can make," he said. At the brewery's sprawling warehouse and taproom visitors can sample the line of beers, mingle among good company, and learn about the history of Mayflower.

Staying true to history, Brosseau recalled the story of how Pilgrims settled at a plantation that had a "very sweet brook" they described as "many delicate springs of as good water as may be drunk." Today, that same water is used to brew the family of Mayflower ales.

Mayflower Brewing Company

Opened: 2008.

Owner: Drew Brosseau.

Brewer: Drew Brosseau.

System: DME 2-vessel 20-barrel brewhouse.

Production: 5,500 barrels in 2011.

Hours: Tuesday through Friday, noon to 6 P.M.; Saturday, 11 A.M. to 3 P.M.

Tours: Thursday and Friday, 4:30 P.M. to 6:30 P.M.; Saturday, 11 A.M. to 3 P.M.

Take-out beer: Growlers, six-packs, and cases.

Extras: Retail store with Mayflower apparel and barware. Facility available for private functions based on schedule.

Parking: On site

Other area beer sites:

- **The British Beer Company** (6 Middle Street, Plymouth, 508-747-1776, www.britishbeer.com) is a chain that serves up decent food and cold pints.
- **The Cabby Shack** (30 Town Wharf, Plymouth, 508-746-5354, www.cabbyshack.com) is a great summer seafood place with a deck overlooking Plymouth harbor.
- **T-Bones Roadhouse** (22 Main Street, Plymouth, 508-747-2667, www.tbonesroadhouse.com) is a large BBQ place in downtown Plymouth and a fun place to eat your fill and get a little crazy.
- **The New World Tavern** (56 Main Street, Plymouth, www.thenewworldtavern.com) is an upscale craft beer bar that recently opened with great promise of elevating the area beer scene.

Salem Beer Works

278 Derby Street, Salem, MA 01970
978-745-2337 • www.beerworks.net

At first glance, the Salem Beer Works is not very different than any of the other four locations in the Beer Works chain (for more on the history of the chain, see Boston Beer Works Canal Street location on page 109). It's a large, cavernous space, with high ceilings, brushed metal, cool wood tones, and smooth poured concrete floors that gives off an almost industrial vibe. But, look a little closer. Head into the dining area near the bar and glance up. Overhead is an enormous neon green silhouette of a witch flying atop a broom—solid proof that you're in Salem, also known as Witch City, U.S.A.

Everyone knows at least a little bit about Salem, the current Halloween capital of the world, beloved by those with a passion for horror stories and any general occult interests. The city is famous as the setting of the witch trials held here in the late seventeenth century, as anyone who has read or seen Arthur Miller's 1953 play *The Crucible* knows.

In May 1692, several local young girls took ill and began having fits: screaming, throwing things, and contorting themselves wildly. A doctor suggested they had been cursed by local witches and the girls went along with the story. A hysteria took over the town, which had been suffering from a dangerous combination of boredom, the traditional strains of living their isolated colonial lifestyle, and extremely strict conservatism, leading the villagers to truly believe the Devil was the cause of all of their ills.

By the end of that one short summer, nearly two hundred people had been accused of vague crimes involving black magic. Nineteen people, mostly women, were hanged on Gallows Hill, several others died in jail, and one seventy-one-year-old man was pressed to death under heavy stones. Not until October were saner voices able to settle down the hysteria and halt the trials. Within ten years, the trials were declared unlawful and restitution was given to the families of those affected, and in 1957, the Commonwealth of Massachusetts issued a formal apology for this part of its history. But Salem is still known as a modern-day precautionary tale against the dangers of allowing paranoia and wild suspicion to overtake calm rationality.

Even though Salem capitalizes off of its haunted history, with no shortage of witch-themed activities, ghost tours, and occult shops, there is a sort of natural creepiness to the city regardless. You can't manufacture the way the fog creeps in from the nearby sea, the gloomy darkness that overtakes the narrow, meandering cobblestoned alleys lined with imposing gothic buildings. We can't imagine a more interesting place to spend a night out drinking with friends, as evidenced by the three separate bachelorette parties that wandered past, dressed in a full-on costumed mix of witch rags and bridal veils, while we were at the bar. And this was only August.

As for the beer? It's the same quality pints we've come to expect from a Beer Works. There is a sense of tradition when it comes to

Beers Brewed: Bunker Hill Blueberry Ale, North Shore Light, Seven Gables Golden, Baker's Island Blond, Victory White, Salem American Pale Ale, Witch City Red, Custom House IPA, Bay State ESB, Hercules Strong Ale, Tell Tale Lager, Black Bay Stout, and a rotating variety of seasonal and specialty beers.

The Pick: Witch City Red—when in Salem, drink in the whimsy.

established styles, but also the creativity that beer geeks crave. Salem is a great town and we're glad it has a deserving brewery.

Salem Beer Works

Opened: 1995.
Owner: Joe Slesar.
Brewers: Zandy Zeiser and Brad Sullivan.
System: 14-barrel Pub system.
Production: 1,000 barrels.
Hours: Daily, 11:30 A.M. to 1 A.M.
Tours: By appointment.
Take-out beer: Growlers and six-packs.
Special considerations: Handicapped-accessible.
Parking: On street.

Cape Ann Brewing Company

11 Rogers Street, Gloucester, MA 01930
978-282-7399 • www.capeannbrewing.com

If the environment you crave is one with salty air, the rythmic lapping sound of water punctuated by the screech of a seagull, or the yell of an angler and the bustling yet serene view of maritime life on a dock, then nothing is better than this waterfront brewery. Add inventive and satisfying pints to the experience and it's about as close to heaven as you can get on this earth.

Cape Ann, which was founded in 2004, moved to its current harbor-side home in 2010 after spending the first six years of its existence across the street in an old factory. This combination brewery and restaurant adapts to the seasons. Warmer months see large windows facing the harbor open wide, allowing for the cooling breeze to come and go freely. A generous awning over the patio keeps off too-harsh sunrays and "deposits" from any resident seagulls. During the harsh winters, the all-wood furniture gives added warmth to the patrons quaffing pints. Its minimalist décor manages to feel intimate.

This new space allowed the brewery to add on a kitchen, and while the menu is rather simple, it's chock-full of the best the ocean's bounty has to offer: mussels steamed in a wheat beer with lemon, chowders, battered and fried fish, crab meat on sandwiches or alone, stuffed clams, and smoked fish. All are delicious and no choice winds up being the wrong one. The new location also allowed for more space for the brewery. With large glass windows that face the street, passersby get a view right into the heart of the action. Lagering tanks on their sides are stacked in the windows pointing their rounded bottoms at the glass.

While he was a homebrewer, Cape Ann owner Jeremy Goldberg had never given much thought to opening a brewery. He was working on Wall Street during the attacks on September 11, 2001, and after escaping the area with so many others he began to reevaluate his life. "I wanted to do more than push money around for other people," Goldberg said. Together with several friends, including Paul Kermizian, one of the owners of the Barcade franchise, he hit the road and visited thirty-eight breweries in forty days. The experience was filmed and released as the 2004 documentary *American Beer*.

When Goldberg returned from the road, he thought about various careers in the beer business, including working with a distributor. His brother-in-law owned a warehouse in Gloucester and his father was looking for a business to invest in. The idea for a brewery was fermented and Cape Ann was born.

Over the years the brewery has seen impressive growth and gained a loyal following. The main brewer, Dylan L'Abbe-Lindquist, along with his team, is turning out impressive and innovative beers, such as a barley wine brewed with three types of tea that were used in the Boston Tea Party or a saison brewed with rhubarb and strawberries. Occasionally one might even find a hefeweizen brewed with pineapples. In October, the Pumpkin Stout doesn't stay on tap or on shelves for very long. In fact, Cape Ann has grown so much that the brewery in Gloucester can only keep up with keg demands. A brewery in Saratoga Springs, New York, handles the bottled offerings.

There are televisions in the bar, but the real entertainment comes from people-watching. Cape Ann is, after all, on a working harbor. In the warmer months, day-trippers, empty coolers in hand, wait to board chartered boats to try their hand at deep-sea fishing. Anglers return

Beers Brewed: Fisherman's Ale, Fisherman's Brew, Fisherman's IPA, Fisherman's Navigator, Fisherman's Pumpkin Stout, Greenhorn Double IPA, Honey Pilsner, 70 Schilling Scottish Ale, Tea Party, Fresh Hop IPA, Home Port, Rock Porter, Sunrise Saison, Imperial Pumpkin Stout, Pick Ale, Fisherman's Bavarian Wheat, Fisherman's Oyster Stout.

The Pick: Fisherman's Oyster Stout is brewed with hundreds of crushed oyster shells placed in the mash, giving this full-bodied stout a salty depth, harmonized with the malty, roasty notes of the grain. Perfect with—you guessed it—freshly shucked oysters. What could be better? Only having the coffee oyster stout on tap!

with the day's catch, some of which winds up on your plate later that night. In the winter, the lobster traps are piled so high on the boardwalk outside of the brewery that the view of the bay is partially obscured.

"People come to the brewery to experience a unique location and have solid craft beers with good food," said Goldberg. But more than that, the brewery is "a community center. We wanted to take the idea of old European breweries and make this a focal point of the community, where people can gather in a beer-hall-style environment, come and get growler fills, have a pint with neighbors, and mingle with tourists over a conversation."

There are subtle nautical trappings throughout the pub, including handmade lures for sale behind the bar and a red channel marker on the left, signaling a return to the harbor. But perhaps the most interesting and pertinent is the photograph hanging on the wall at the far end of the bar. It's a shot of the schooner *Harry L. Belden*, taken at the turn of the twentieth century. The vessel is famous for having won the Fisherman's Race, celebrating the 250th anniversary of Gloucester, held in such windy conditions that it was nicknamed "the race it blew." What's of real interest in the picture, however, is what's on shore behind the boat—the Amber Brewing Company. It only survived from 1898 to 1902, but it is clearly depicted on a now-gone pier just down the street from where Cape Ann now operates. The brewery was in production that day, with water clearly coming from the building and the words "Real Ale" printed on its side.

It is a great reminder of the proud brewing history this city has known on many levels and a sign of the great things still to come.

Cape Ann Brewing Company

Opened: 2004.

Owners: Jeremy and Michael Goldberg.

Brewers: Jeremy Goldberg, Dylan L'Abbe Lindquist, and Brian Fines

System: 20-barrel.

Production: 2,700 barrels in 2011.

Hours: Daily, 11 A.M. to midnight.

Tours: On request.

Take-out beer: Growlers.

Extras: Tuesday, Sing Along Sea Shanties; Wednesday, trivia night; Thursday, Open Mic. Live music. Cape Ann merchandise available, including T-shirts, hoodies, caps, visors, pint glasses, and mugs.

Special considerations: Handicapped-accessible.

Parking: Public lot next door.

Hingham Beer Works

18 Shipyard Drive, Hingham, MA 02043
781-749-2337 • www.beerworks.net

Located inside a shopping and entertainment complex along the shoreline in this naval-minded city, Hingham Beer Works is part of the Beer Works chain that has two locations in Boston, one in Lowell, and another in Salem. For more on the history of the chain, check out the Boston Beer Works Canal Street location on page 109.

Like the others, the Hingham location has a modern feel with brushed metal and cool woods. The two-tier brewing system, encased in glass, sits directly behind the main bar, giving it an imposing feel.

We've focused on the beer in other Beer Works entries, but it is worth mentioning the food as well. It's a pubcentric, family-friendly option for those looking for a burger, pizza, or just a snack. We enjoyed the pretzel bites that came out hot and fluffy with huge grains of salt. There is heartier fare like ribs, meatloaf dinners, and swordfish steak. It has something for everyone and offers a good meal for the price.

This is the newest location in the local chain and on several visits, it was nice to see tables packed and pints hoisted by people relaxing after an afternoon of shopping or waiting for a movie.

Beers Brewed: Bunker Hill Blueberry Ale, Minot Light, Baker's Island Blond, Mayflower Maybock, Hingham Pale Ale, World's End IPA, Back River Red, Telltale Lager, Hooligan Ale, Curley's Irish Stout, and a rotating variety of seasonal and specialty beers.

The Pick: The Double Pale Ale can seem like a gimmick (and it likely is), but this beer is hoppier than a normal pale, but not quite as hoppy as an IPA. Just the right bite makes you want another after the first.

Hingham Beer Works

Opened: 2010.

Owner: Joe Slesar.

Brewers: Tim Wilson and Josh Sattin.

System: 10-barrel Newlands.

Production: 1,200 barrels.

Hours: Daily, 11:30 A.M. to 1 A.M.

Tours: By request.

Take-out beer: Growlers and six-packs.

Special considerations: Handicapped-accessible.

Parking: Ample.

Brewing Beer

At its core, beer consists of just four ingredients: water, grain, hops, and yeast. It is, however, how those four are mixed, tinkered with, and fermented that can be the difference between a great brew and one not even suitable to water plants.

When you visit the breweries mentioned in this book you'll see a lot of equipment of varying sizes. Most of it will be made of stainless steel and full of beer in some stage of the brewing process.

So, how is beer made? It starts out with the grain. Depending on the recipe or style, a variety of grains can be used. The whole grains are put through a gristmill that cracks and opens the grain, separating the husk from the interior. From there, it is transported to the mash tun, where it is mixed with hot water (upwards of 155 degrees), and steeps for a while. During this process sugars in the grain are broken down, which will later turn this mix into alcohol.

From there, a thick oatmeal-like substance, called wort, develops. The liquid is drained from the mash tun and transferred into a brew kettle.

According to industry statistics, by the way, most of the barley malt grown in the country goes to feed livestock. Only a small portion goes into brewing. With this in mind, many breweries donate their spent grain to local farmers to be used as feed. Lucky animals!

Anyway, once the liquid is in the brew kettle, it is brought to a boil and hops are added at different intervals. Most boils last about ninety minutes but can go for more or less time with some recipes. Depending on the style, different hop varieties can be added. When they are added and for how long will affect the end result, of course. And brewers have a lot of fun experimenting during this step.

After the boil, the brew is brought through a heat exchanger that cools down the wort and the liquid is emptied into a fermentation tank. It's at this step that the brewer's yeast is added. There are thousands of strains of yeast and, again, depending on the style of beer, a different strain can be added. The yeast feasts upon the sugars in the wort, creating alcohol and CO_2, or beer.

But the process is not over yet. While some will use fermentation tanks for aging, others will use bright beer or conditioning tanks, in which the beer can mature and strengthen for weeks, months, or even a year, depending on what the brewer is looking for.

Before the beer is transferred to serving tanks, it is usually filtered. Some beers, like wheat beers, skip this step because the haze is part of the allure and style guidelines. Other beers, like pale ale, should be clear.

Once in the serving tanks, the fun really begins. The tanks are connected to the taps behind a bar, or used to fill kegs, growlers, bottles, cans, or anything else one would use to transport beer.

This is, of course, a simplified version of how to make beer. The process can vary from brewery to brewery. Some places will use malt extract, skipping the milling process. And the four ingredients that we mentioned are not the only things that one can put in beer. Virtually any edible or drinkable thing a person can think of can be added to a brew. Again, some work better than others.

Some breweries try to keep it pure by following the *Reinheitsgebot*, a nearly five-hundred-year-old law that once dictated that German beer be made with just water, barley, and hops (yeast came later).

The bottom line is that the majority of beers being produced in the United States by craft brewers are of exceptional quality. Most brewers have gone through formal training and likely have an extensive home-brewing background. Like chefs, they experiment and try to find a recipe that will play well in their area. That's why an IPA made in Washington State will vary from one produced in, say, New Jersey.

Of course taste accounts for something. We've been at brewpubs and breweries where people will have wildly different reactions to the same beer. In reality, both are right. No one knows your tastes like you.

If you want to learn more about the brewing process or brewing at home there are a variety of resources that can teach you how to do it and find vendors that sell equipment that can fill a garage or take up a corner in an apartment closet.

And should you choose to go that route, you'll experience a great sense of pride and accomplishment and a better understanding of the fermented beverage in your glass. And, you'll have something to talk about with the brewer at your local establishment next time you visit.

Cape Cod and the Islands

Cape Cod. Martha's Vineyard. Nantucket. The words alone conjure up images of gentle New England beaches, nautical striped shirts, rolling dunes, and breezy sea grass. But as much as the area is known for its graceful beauty and old-timey ambiance, it's also known for its history. Just five minutes spent walking on Nantucket's cobblestoned streets will bridge the gap between the present day and the mid-nineteenth century, when whaling was a boom industry and street after street of this salty old town was lined with clapboard captain's houses with widow's walks on their peaks.

The three areas are similar in their general landscape and of course have much in common, but are worlds apart when it comes to the smaller details.

Cape Cod juts out from mainland Massachusetts, famously shaped like an arm flexed to show off a bicep. It has meandering coastlines and many, many individual communities from the moment you cross the Cape Cod Canal (at the shoulder) all the way to Provincetown (the fingertips) perched on the final edge. It's made up of a mix of year-round residents (roughly 230,000) and of course, the many thousands more who descend upon the area in the summer months. This mix of regular communities combined with summery tourist attractions make this a great place to both live and visit. You can spend the day in total vacation mode—sailing, relaxing on the beach, or biking—and then top off the night with a beachside clambake. Or, you can just as easily hop in the car and head to the nearest strip mall to buy light bulbs, or any other basic things you might need, in your regular workaday life. This is a place that has everything.

Cape Cod has more towns than you can shake a stick at, all with their own unique twist or claim to fame, but some of course are more popular than others. The heavy-hitter is Hyannis, located Mid-Cape, and home to the famous Kennedy compound. This is where everyone flocks to enjoy great restaurants and nightlife or to just pop in and out of touristy shops for souvenirs. It's got a great main drag for wandering and soaking up the rich atmosphere, and is also a place to catch a ferry to the neighboring islands.

Another great spot and arguably just as well known is Province-town, ("P-Town" to locals) on the very edge of the Cape. This village is a bustling artistic community as well as a famous gay and lesbian mecca. Its nontraditional downtown is lined with great hotels, restaurants, cafes, and shops and looks out toward the wilds of the cold Atlantic. But outside of all that bustle are enormous, lunarlike sand dunes and empty plains of beach grass that evoke a desolate, world's edge kind of beauty.

But the Cape is a mix of dozens of fabulous little enclaves worth your time and attention. Some smaller, but favorite, ones of ours are lovely Harwich Port, with its sleepy downtown and calm bay beaches, or quaint Chatham, where you can grab a great lunch and wander the main drag in search of beachy gifts for whoever you left at home. There truly is a community for any mood here and outdoor activities for every interest, with bike trails, hiking, and opportunities for swimming in quiet bays or on the wilder ocean side, and restaurants for every style and budget. But most valuable of all is the sensation that you have the ability to get away from it all here, if you want, or the sense of neighborhood, community, and opportunities for a year-round lifestyle.

Worlds away, although only seven miles by ferry, is beautiful Martha's Vineyard. Immediately upon arrival we realized this was more of a vacation-only mindset. There are plenty of options to get here via ferry, and we took the Hy-Line, a quick one-hour ride from Hyannis for $29 one way. As you disembark on a creaky dock in Oak Bluffs, you immediately see a couple of salty, old-fashioned casual bars, an ice cream shop or two, and within one short block, the heart of downtown. If you're vacationing there's no need for a car here, and most people shun them. This is a place where people come to really unplug, and while residents do live here year-round, there are only 15,000 of them as compared to the summer swell of up to 125,000 in July and August. Those that do live here year-round work almost exclusively in the tourism and service industries, or in peripheral ones such as farming or fishing, which support the local economy (and all those seasonal visitors) as they arrive.

The island is ninety-six square miles of picturesque beauty, with gentle beaches and a smattering of towns. It's divided into "up-island" and "down-island," with up-island made up of primarily rural farming communities and down-island where more visitors land. Three major towns make up the down-island area. Oak Bluffs is arguably the best known, a friendly, seafaring town of cute shops, streets lined with storefronts, easy access to ferry service and beaches, and open rolling parks. You can also head into the artsy town of Vineyard Haven for a more bohemian-style vacation, or go to Edgartown, the more sophisticated and chic of the three towns, for more high-end dining and accommodation options and boutique shopping.

Martha's Vineyard's has a reputation as a place where rich people vacation, where presidents visit to "get away from it all," and while that's true, it does retain a softer, more family-oriented and casual side that really is inviting. In fact, only three sitting presidents have vacationed here—Barack Obama, Bill Clinton, and surprisingly, Ulysses S. Grant. The story goes that when Oak Bluffs was home to a conservative Methodist revival camp back in the mid-nineteenth century, sitting president Grant attended church with the community and family during the day, but by night, snuck outside of the gated religious community to visit the local taverns that had inevitably sprung up outside. Unfortunately, he was over-served, and by the time he wandered back to the camp he found himself locked out, and was forced to spend the night outside the gates sleeping it off.

Even now people get into the presidential spirit. When the Obamas came to town in the summer of 2011, Offshore Ale of Oaks Bluffs celebrated with their own Ale to the Chief, and a neighborhood Mexican joint served up Obamaritas.

Last up, and farthest away, is Nantucket, a wild twenty-three miles from the nearest land and truly isolated. Nantucket was world-famous in the mid-nineteenth century for its whaling history. Ships would dock here after spending months at sea to drop off both whales and crew members. Then the captains (and their money) would head for their stately homes and quieter, more refined lives in Martha's Vineyard, leaving Nantucket to do the dirty work of processing the whales for oil. But Nantucket profited from this trade immensely, and a beautiful town sprung up to support the industry and its workers.

Whaling soon became unsustainable, and when new methods of finding oil came into play Nantucket began to fold back into oblivion. But in recent decades it's been rediscovered as a tourist destination for its well-maintained homes, beautifully preserved downtown, and wild beaches. While indisputably beautiful, it's also very pricey, with a plethora of bed-and-breakfasts, designer shops, high-end restaurants, and luxury hotels. It has a beachy-luxury vibe, and is utterly preppy and very old money New England, but still truly nautical, historical, and with a wild beauty that keeps people visiting again and again.

There is an endless supply of great restaurants on Cape Cod, everything from clam shacks to four-star dining experiences. One trick to finding the best in your area is to ask a local where they like to go in the off-season. That's usually a sign that it stands among the best. Not to be missed are the breakfast pastries known as meltaways, which have a Danish-like appearance but are so sweet that they melt in your mouth. Get them to go from Bonatt's Bakery & Restaurant (537 Rte. 28, Harwich Port, 508-423-7199).

Cape Cod has an almost unimaginable variety of places to lay your head. Here are some favorites.

- **Land's End** (www.landsendinn.com), in Provincetown, is a secluded inn overlooking the ocean.

- **SeaCoast Inn** (www.seacoastcapecod.com), in downtown Hyannis, is most affordable.

- **Shoreway Acres Inn** (www.shorewayacresinn.com), in Falmouth, is a family-friendly and affordable inn spread out on a sprawling property dotted with townhouses, within easy walking distance of both the downtown and the beach.

- **The Island Inn** (www.islandinn.com), on Martha's Vineyard, is located just across from the ocean on the outskirts of Oak Bluffs on a sprawling pocket of land scattered with cottages and the large main building. With tennis courts, a freshwater pool, and a picnic and barbeque area, you won't even have to leave the hotel grounds to enjoy the great outdoors that make Martha's Vineyard so appealing.

- **Harbor View Hotel and Resort** (www.harbor-view.com), in Edgartown, is a historic hotel located right on the waterfront, with lots of great amenities and a comfortable ambience.

- **Hawthorn House** (www.hawthornhouse.com), in Nantucket, is easy on the wallet and is a small-ish but beautiful private home located in the heart of downtown, within walking distance of shops, restaurants, and ferry docks.

- **White Elephant** (www.whiteelephanthotel.com), situated on Nantucket Harbor and an island landmark since the 1920s, is luxurious and the place to go if money is no object.

If you're in the area, chances are you're looking to spend your time outdoors. While on Cape Cod, you might want to rent a couple of bikes to take in the scenery on the area's mostly flat and fairly easy trails. Some good ones are Shining Sea Bikeway, a four-mile trail along the shoreline in the Falmouth area, and the Cape Cod Rail Trail, which runs through thirty miles of wooded conservation lands. Here are some other area activities.

- **Cape Cod National Seashore** (www.nps.gov/caco) is the place to go to spend the day relaxing in the sun. It has forty miles of unspoiled beaches, marshes, ponds, and trails set aside as conservation lands. It is also home to Marconi Beach, named for the Italian inventor who successfully completed the first transatlantic wireless communication between the United States and England in 1903.

- **Provincetown Whale Watch** (www.provincetownwhalewatch.com) can't be beat for a good value, and the company has lots of well-earned experience.

- **Island Spirit Kayak** (www.islandspiritkayak.com) on Martha's Vineyard is the place for kayaking and to get some fresh air while exploring the local wildlife.

- **Nantucket Whaling Museum** (www.nha.org) is where you can view a huge life-sized whale skeleton and learn about the island's whaling heyday.

Cape Cod Beer

"A Vacation In Every Pint"

1336 Phinney's Lane, Hyannis, MA 02601
508-790-4200 • www.capecodbeer.com

It was a Friday and the clock struck noon. The doors of Cape Cod Beer opened for business and within three minutes there was a line six people deep waiting to get growlers filled, purchasing new ones, returning kegs, and picking up new orders. Still more people were browsing the shelves of locally made merchandise and at least one gentleman was in the homebrew section thinking about his next recipe.

Through the glass doors separating the brewhouse from the retail shop came Todd Marcus, the owner and brewer of this near-perfect representation of a small brewery. The professional road to this one-story, aluminum-sided building on Phinney's Lane, a short drive from the well-heeled sidewalks of Hyannis's downtown, had quite a few brewery stops along the way.

A Massachusetts native, Marcus earned his degree in electrical engineering from New Jersey's Stevens Institute of Technology and after graduation found himself back in the Bay State working for an engineering firm. He was homebrewing at the time and had a colleague with a family business in stainless steel. At that time in the mid-1990s there was growing concern in the brewing industry about using brass and many were switching to stainless. The colleague saw a niche opportunity, and one evening headed to a brewer's club meeting at Redbones in Somerville to pitch his wares. He invited Marcus along, and within just a few minutes the young homebrewer realized he was among friends and peers. He quit his job the very next morning and focused on becoming a professional brewer.

His first professional stop was the still newish Long Trail Brewing Company in Vermont. As should be the case with first-time brewery employees, Marcus was put to work washing kegs and working in the cellar. It was a great introduction to life at a midsized brewery and while there he learned the importance of quality and consistency. In 1996, he got a job at Sandy River Brewing in Bethel, Maine. Two weeks after he arrived as an assistant brewer, the head brewer left, leaving Marcus to a baptism by fire. During that busy ski season he learned all about the brewpub environment and was able to hone recipes by directly interacting with customers at the bar.

He married longtime sweetheart Beth in 1997, all while opening up a John Harvard's Brew House in Springfield, Pennsylvania. The ribbon-cutting was two days after the wedding, and Marcus says he still owes his bride a proper honeymoon. He was able to learn the corporate environment at Harvard's and see the real work that goes into opening a brewery from the ground up.

While Pennsylvania was fine enough, Todd and Beth began hearing the siren call of Massachusetts. They wanted to be closer to family and return to their roots a bit. During a visit to the Great American

Beers Brewed: Amber Ale, India Pale Ale, Beach Blonde Ale, Summer, Harvest, Porter, Dunkel, Berry Merry Holiday Ale, Old Man Winter.

The Pick: Christmas in July is it. Each year Todd makes a 7.5 percent ABV old ale called Old Man Winter. It is, clearly, released in the dead of winter. But then he reserves a bit, ages it on oak, and releases it in the summer for their Christmas in July. It's malty and robust and worth looking forward to all year long.

Beer Festival in 1998, he mentioned this to a friend who turned him on to an opportunity in Hyannis on Cape Cod. Soon enough he found himself brewing in a 500-square-foot brewhouse attached to a restaurant. Over the next few years, the management floundered and the place changed names a few times (Hyannis Port Brewing Company and then HyPort Brewing Company), but Marcus continued to make good beer for eager customers.

In 2004, Marcus leased equipment space from the brewery and launched Cape Cod Beer. He started out with twelve accounts and by the time the adjoining restaurant finally closed he was distributing to forty clients. Soon after, he moved and was brewing inside this 5,000-square-foot space. Today he and Beth have seventeen employees on the payroll and are supplying more than 350 accounts with Cape Cod. "We're available from Plymouth to P-Town," he told us.

In just a few short years they have become a distinctive Cape Cod product. And while they haven't quite fully penetrated the market, Marcus said they have focused on year-round accounts that continually serve their beer. In fact, it's somewhat difficult to find a bar on the Cape that doesn't carry their beer. In a place known for vacations, Marcus built a twelve-month mentality into his business plan. Accounting for leaner times in cold-weather months has allowed the brewery to expand with unanticipated extra cash that comes in the summer.

Todd and Beth like to keep their footprint small. The brewery sells refillable growlers and kegs to customers. Swing-top bottles are available for sale for people who want to bring a souvenir home from vacation, but they have shunned nonrefillable packaging. The Cape is an environmentally conscious place, and at the brewery, recycling is taken very seriously, to the point where they only generate a bag of trash per week.

They also care about fellow businesses on the Cape. Just about everything for sale in their gift shop is made on the Cape or utilizes a local business (their durable T-shirts are made off the Cape, but embroidered nearby). Almost everything in their retail shop is local, including Cape Cod Potato Chips, but only the ones made in Hyannis, not at other factories around the country. Todd estimates that seventy-five cents of every dollar sold in the store goes to a Cape business.

The brewery offers full tours on weekends, but for those who pop in for a spontaneous visit, there is a self-guided option. A roped-off area inside the brewery shows the various ingredients, tells the Cape Cod Beer story, and gives guests a spot at the bar for some samples.

With its location in a vacation town, the brewery finds itself doing a lot of education. When they first launched with two beers—the Red and the IPA—the brewery requested that bartenders serve the Red first, and explain the ingredients and flavors to customers, fearing that a hoppy IPA would turn people off the brand forever. It was an extra effort, but a necessary one. They've since added more beers to the regular and seasonal lineup, including the Beach Blonde Ale that appeases the "what's your lightest beer?" crowd. Interestingly, the blonde tap markers are made from reclaimed driftwood and laser etched by the good folks at the Barnstable Bat Company.

Another thing that Cape Cod Beer does well and correctly is social media. Beth gives restaurant recommendations (most happen to serve Cape Cod Beer) and paints a picture of life on the Cape that serves as a handy year-round guide for visitors. There have been at least two other companies that used the name Cape Cod Beer. The first one, from the 1940s and 1950s, is long gone, but for those who collect breweriana, cans that display the logo from that era can fetch upwards of $1,000 each. The second incarnation known as Cape Cod Brand Beer (the brand is almost too small to read on packaging) came along in the 1970s and had a kitschy label reminiscent of a cartoon map postcard. The ale was brewed in a long-defunct brewery in New Jersey and packaged in stub bottles, like Red Stripe. Todd said people show up with those bottles now and again at the brewery, but when they pop them open they haven't held up well. "It tastes like vinegar," he told us.

But Todd and Beth were the first to trademark the name and certainly have the talent, determination, and loyal following to make their version of Cape Cod Beer the best and longest-lasting incarnation.

Cape Cod Beer

Opened: 2004.

Owners: Todd and Beth Marcus.

Brewers: Todd Marcus, brewmaster; Ron Cotti, operations manager; and Brain Flagg, James Moriarty, and Corey Peterson, brewers.

System: 15-barrel direct-fired Premier Stainless Brewhouse.

Production: 4,200 barrels in 2011.

Hours: Monday through Friday, noon to 6 P.M.; Saturday 11 A.M. to 2 P.M.

Tours: Tuesday, 11 A.M.; Saturday, 1 P.M.

Take-out beer: Growlers and kegs.

Extras: Happy hours. Live music. Retail shop sells glasses, hats, and T-shirts, as well as a wide selection of products made on Cape Cod and products made with Cape Cod Beer, including beer brittle and spent-grain bread.

Special considerations: Handicapped-accessible. Please let the brewery know if special accommodation is needed. They are more than happy to facilitate you to the best of their ability.

Parking: On site.

Other area beer sites:

- **Nor'East Beer Garden** (266 Commercial Street, Provincetown, 508-487-2337, www.noreastbeergarden.com) has possibly one of the most inspired beer lineups in the area and a locally sourced menu to match.

- **The Squealing Pig** (335 Commercial Street, Provincetown, 508-487-5804, www.squealingpigptown.com) has a great beer list and oyster bar, and it also features live music from a variety of bands, including our pal Nate Schweber and his roots-rock band The New Heathens.

- **Flynn's Irish Pub** (119 Cranberry Highway, Buzzard's Bay, 508-833-8626, www.gotoflynns.com) had been voted one of the top places to have a pint by the *Cape Cod Times*, and indeed it is just that.

- **British Beer Company** has several locations on the Cape, serving decent pub food and cold pints (Hyannis Port, Falmouth, and Sandwich, www.britishbeer.com).

- **Grain & Vine** (101 Iyannough Road, Hyannis Port, 508-775-0660, www.grainandvine.com) has more than 350 beers, a wonderful wine selection, and whiskey too! It's the place to go to stock the vacation house.

Cisco Brewers

5 Bartlett Farm Road, Nantucket, MA 02554
508-325-5929 • www.ciscobrewers.com

Call it an estate, call it a campus, or just call it a great place to visit, Cisco is a hat trick. Along with the brewery, the grounds are home to Nantucket Vineyards and Triple Eight Distillery. Each is housed in its own building and has its own tasting room and shop. The doors open to a brick-and-cobblestone courtyard with tables and benches where local salty fishermen and madras-wearing preppy tourists mix, each drinking the local libation of their choosing. The distillery is likely the most popular, with everything from Bloody Marys to straight whiskey being served. The winery room is what you would expect from vino tasters: swirling, sipping, and spitting. The brewery room is a lot of fun. It's not uncommon for customers to be lined up six deep at the small bar. Naturally, that's where we spent most of our time.

We watched as expert bartender and affable host Tracy Wilde Long expertly walked customers through the lineup of beers. With the enthusiasm of a cheerleader she explained the Woods (barrel-aged sour beers), and given the season, pumpkin beers on tap. Old favorites like the Sankaty Light and Whale's Tale Pale Ale were also in fashion and poured with vigor and skill.

It was a Saturday in autumn when we last visited and although it was technically the off-season you would never know it, given the amount of people streaming in and joining Jeffrey Horner, the brewer, on a tour of the facilities.

There are two tour rules, announced Horner, a man with muttonchops and a welcoming attitude. The first is that guests are encouraged to interrupt the spiel at any time with questions. The second is that a glass is never allowed to be empty. As if by wizardry, growlers appeared with everything from the unfiltered Belgian-style wheat ale known as Grey Lady to their Very Brown IPA, a tongue-in-cheek nod to the emerging style known as Black IPA or Cascadian Dark Ale. Contents were tipped into glasses and Horner would spend the next hour or so talking about the brewing equipment (they also brew at two locations on the mainland), the winery, and the distillery, where things wrapped up with a taste of jalapeño pineapple vodka. It can be difficult to make it through the tour with a clear head, but all things in moderation. Be cautioned that heavy mixing of all three drinks can lead to a less than enthusiastic start to tomorrow.

After visiting Nantucket, it's clear to see why some people would want to put down roots here. In the case of Dean and Melissa Long, the desire was to plant grapes, and so in 1981, they founded the Nantucket Vineyard. They hoped to create wines with native grapes, but the local weather made that impossible, so now wines are made on the island with the choicest grapes selected from around the country.

A little more than a decade later Randy and Wendy Hudson came together on the island and formed a working relationship with Dean and Melissa. They moved to the property, worked for the business, and opened a brewery.

Beers Brewed: Whale's Tale Pale Ale, Sankaty Light Lager, The Grey Lady, Captain Swain's Extra Stout, India Pale Ale, Bailey's Blonde Ale, Summer of Lager , Moor Porter, Baggywrinkle Barleywine, Very Brown IPA, Pumple Drumkin, The Woods, Winter Woods, Monomoy Kriek, Full & By Rye, Lady of the Woods, Cherry Woods, Island Reserve Smoked "Top Notch" Pumpkin.

The Pick: The Island Reserve Smoked "Top Notch" Pumpkin is as creative as it is lip-smacking. Brewed with Bartlett pumpkins and whiskey staves in the mash, the grain was smoked using a whiskey barrel from the distillery that was no longer useable. Its loss is our gain.

After a few years, Jay Harmon came on. He was a college student when Randy and Wendy met him, working on a business plan and contemplating opening his own brewery on the island. It was a happy occasion of join them rather than beat them, and Harmon in his role as brewery CEO has been a tireless proponent of the operation. A brewery tale is told that he capped sixty thousand bottles of beer during his first summer with the company—no small task.

As the business grew and the need for more space became apparent, Cisco expanded and Dean had the foresight to build a distillery, named Triple Eight. They are known for their vodkas, with flavors like cranberry and blueberry, but their rum and bourbon are also sought. Both, by the way, clock in at 88.8 proof.

Cisco is like an adult amusement park without the rides (unless you're lucky enough to get a lift in their refurbished VW van) and after just a few minutes with a drink in hand it's clear to see why it is one of the most popular spots on the island.

Another great thing about Cisco is its location. A seven-minute car ride, fifteen-minute bike ride, or forty-minute walk outside of the village, it gives visitors a chance to see more of the island and discover an oasis among farmland. "This is a great place, isn't it?" asked Harmon as the night wound down. "It's unlike anything else." We couldn't agree more.

Cisco Brewers

Opened: 1995.

Owners: Randy Hudson, Wendy Hudson, Jay Harman, Dean Long, and Melissa Long.

Brewers: Jeff Horner and Ian Spencer.

System: 15-barrel.

Production: 2,200 barrels in 2011.

Tours: Daily at 4 P.M.

Take-out beer: Growlers

Special considerations: Handicapped-accessible.

Parking: Limited. Consider renting a bike or taking a taxi.

Other area beer sites:

- **The Brotherhood of Thieves** (23 Broad Street, Nantucket, 508-228-2551, www.brotherhoodofthieves.com) is a fun bar with good food and is frequented by great people.

Offshore Ale Company

30 Kennebec Avenue, Oak Bluffs, MA 02557
508-693-2626 • www.offshoreale.com

For those who hear the call of the island, there is nothing to do but heed the voices. Such was the fate that Phil and Colleen McAndrews found themselves living after visiting Martha's Vineyard years ago while on vacation. Hearing the call, by all accounts, is a wonderful thing.

Although he had spent summers vacationing on Nantucket, Phil and Colleen had not spent much time in the area after that. That changed with a 2005 vacation when, before heading home, they already started contemplating full-time island life. They looked around and Phil, who worked as a beer, wine, and spirits salesman, heard that Offshore Ale was for sale. "We said 'yeah, this is it' and six months later had picked up stakes and moved here," he told us over beers in his second-floor office at the brewery on a busy post-summer night. "It was kind of an impulse buy."

But what a deal it was. The brewery, founded in 1997, was practically walk-in ready when Phil and Colleen arrived. It makes the most of the space it has and combines the feeling of a lodge with a dry dock. One would expect a nautical theme, but this is tasteful, not tacky. Warm wood paneling helps keep the din of conversation down when the place is packed—as it often is. Nautical flags line the walls and above are small boats, permanently out of the water, but helping to set the tone. There are only two televisions in this bar, giving locals and visitors a chance to catch the game and discuss the finer points of rivalries between Boston-based teams and those from other cities. However, since it is one of the few establishments that remain open all year long (the previous owner closed for a few weeks in winter), it is mostly about community, stability, and familiarity.

Beers Brewed: Hop Goddess, Menemsha Creek Pale Ale, India Pale Ale, East Chop Lighthouse, Beach Road Brown Ale, Offshore IPA, Steeprock Stout, Islander Double IPA, Black Point Porter, Abel's Hill India Dark, Offshore Amber, Merseyside Red Ale, Flying Monkey, Cascadian Dark IPA, Inkwell Imperial Stout, Blueberry Ale, Mann Hutte, Oktoberfest.

The Pick: For several summers the Obama family visited Martha's Vineyard for an annual summer vacation. Offshore Ales commemorated the visit by releasing Ale to the Chief, a pale ale made from all American ingredients. Give this tasty brew a try.

Since it is a brewery, it's also about the beer. So, let's talk about that for a few moments. Through the able talents of Neil Atkins, who cut his teeth at California's Anderson Valley Brewing Company, customers can quaff pints that draw from Belgian, English, and American brewing traditions. We particularly enjoyed a fresh hop beer with the title ingredient provided by local beer enthusiasts who grew the flowers on the island's Hopp Farm Road. The Hop Goddess, a Belgian-meets-American style IPA, was another hit.

Atkins has also learned to cater to the needs and wants of customers. After a day of brewing he's able to pull up a stool at the bar and talk beer. There he can learn palates, see firsthand what sells best, and can formulate a strategy. It's like an ultimate focus group with near-instant results. As such, the brewery has added a gold and an amber to the lineup, part of pleasing customers not familiar with craft beer, but also keeping them from leaving to find something more familiar. "He's a special character," McAndrews said of Atkins, "and a hell of a brewer."

The brew system is a European design that takes up two stories, with the brewhouse and fermentation tanks above, and serving tanks behind the glass-walled bar. For those into unique systems, this is one to check out.

McAndrews calls the brewery "the mother ship," like it's a hub of all things. And in many respects it is. Along with food and drink (they also have an impressive wine list) there is live music on weekends, where they push tables out of the way and let people sing along and dance. Look closely when Auntie Em and the Bedspins are playing, and you're likely to see the owner himself performing.

There is something immediately comfortable about the overall brewery. It's the great smell of wood-oven pizza and fresh steamed mussels coming from the kitchen, the sound of clinking pints and scraping forks. And the small touches like a barrel of shuck-yourself peanuts by the door, giving waiting patrons more to do than play with their cell phones. The friendly and attentive staff plays a key role as well. Offshore feels like a place you've visited before, even if it's your first time, and that lets you settle into a vacation frame of mind.

While tourism is the bread and butter for island business, McAndrews says he never forgets his full-time neighbors. "We're always going to be respectful of the community, because we're all in this together."

The Offshore Ale Company

Opened: 1997.

Owner: Phil McAndrews.

Brewer: Neil Atkins.

System: 10-barrel Liquid Assets.

Production: 600 barrels in 2011.

Hours: Daily, 11:30 A.M. to midnight.

Tours: On request.

Take-out beer: Growlers.

Extras: Frequent live music. Dining specials in the off-season. Offshore merchandise available, including hats, hoodies, T-shirts, and pint glasses.

Special considerations: Handicapped-accessible.

Parking: Not available. It is recommended that visitors leave their cars on the mainland.

Beerwebs

As the American Craft Beer Movement has grown, so too has the number of websites dedicated to breweries, beer, and the people who brew it. Everything is out there, from sites that review beers one by one to those that provide beer and food pairings and detailed histories. It can be difficult to separate the wheat from the chaff, so here are a few of our own suggestions to help navigate the world of online beer.

Beer Briefing
www.beerbriefing.com
This is a shameless plug for John's website, which includes musings, reviews, and links to beer articles. Updates on Massachusetts breweries will be posted to this site.

Massachusetts Brewers Guild
www.massbrewersguild.com
This online home to the state guild has news, events, and other relevant information from its member breweries.

CraftBeer
www.craftbeer.com
The Brewer's Association, a group that represents the roughly 2,000 microbreweries, brewpubs, and craft breweries in the United States, runs this site, which offers profiles of brewing professionals, recipes and beer pairings, and news from around the brewing world.

Ale Street News Online
www.alestreetnews.com
Ale Street News is the country's largest-circulation beer newspaper. The website includes commentary, news, and insight from every corner of the brewing world.

BeerAdvocate
www.beeradvocate.com
This is one of the better places on the web for people to come together to rate and discuss beer. Opinions run the gamut at this site and can

serve as a good introduction to a certain style or a definitive guide for a particular beer.

Seen through a Glass: Lew Bryson's Beer and Whiskey Blog
www.lewbryson.com
The man who wrote the first three books in the Breweries Series for Stackpole Books maintains a home on the Internet. It's clear to see why Lew Bryson is one of the most celebrated beer writers in the country. His writing is full of quick thoughts, well-rationalized arguments, and slices of everyday life. Visit once and you'll be hooked.

Appellation Beer
http://appellationbeer.com
Esteemed beer writer Stan Hieronymus maintains this online home for his writings. The comments section is usually full of intelligent discussion.

2 Beer Guys
http://2beerguys.com
Through reviews, brewery visits, and discussions with industry folks, this site is the North Shore's definitive source for craft beer education. The two guys have amassed quite a bit of knowledge.

BeerNews
www.beernews.org
Editor Adam Nason posts federally approved beer labels long before they hit the bottle, giving readers an inside look at what's to come. Articles are posted that gives great insight to the stories behind the beers. This is a must-read site for beer geeks.

Glossary

The following list of terms has been excerpted from the fourth edition of Lew Bryson's *Pennsylvania Breweries*.

ABV/ABW. Alcohol by volume/alcohol by weight. These are two slightly different ways of measuring the alcohol content of beverages, as a percentage of either the beverage's total volume or its weight. For example, if you have 1 liter of 4 percent ABV beer, 4 percent of that liter (40 milliliters) is alcohol. However, because alcohol weighs only 79.6 percent as much as water, that same beer is only 3.18 percent ABW. This may seem like a dry exercise in mathematics, but it is at the heart of the common misconception that Canadian beer is stronger than American beer. Canadian brewers generally use ABV figures, whereas American brewers have historically used the lower ABW figures. Mainstream Canadian and American lagers are approximately equal in strength. Just to confuse the issue further, most American microbreweries use ABV figures. This is very important if you're trying to keep a handle on how much alcohol you're consuming. If you know how much Bud (at roughly 5 percent ABV) you can safely consume, you can extrapolate from there. Learn your limits . . . before you hit them.

Adjunct. Any nonbarley malt source of sugars for fermentation. This can be candy sugar, corn grits, corn or rice syrups, or one of any number of specialty grains. Wheat, rye, and candy sugars are considered by beer geeks to be "politically correct" adjuncts; corn and rice are generally taken as signs of swill. Small amounts of corn and rice, however, used as brewing ingredients for certain styles of beer, are slowly gaining acceptance in craft-brewing circles. Try to keep an open mind.

Ale. The generic term for warm-fermented beers.

ATTTB. The federal Alcohol and Tobacco Tax and Trade Bureau, formerly part of the ATF, a branch of the Treasury Department. The ATTTB is the federal regulatory arm for the brewing industry. It has to inspect every brewery before it opens, approve every label before it is used, and approve all packaging. The ATTTB is also the body responsible for the fact that while every food, even bottled water, *must have* a nutritional information label, beer (and wine and cider and spirits) is *not allowed* to have one, even though it is a significant source of calories, carbohydrates, and in the case of unfiltered beers, B vitamins and protein. The bureau has become much more cooperative with the craft beer industry, presumably because they've recognized that it's not going away.

Barley. A wonderfully apt grain for brewing beer. Barley grows well in relatively marginal soils and climates. It has no significant gluten content, which makes it unsuitable for baking bread and thereby limits market competition for brewers buying the grain. Its husk serves as a very efficient filter at the end of the mashing process. And it makes beer that tastes really, really good. The grain's kernels, or corns, are the source of the name "John Barleycorn," a traditional personification of barley or beer.

Barrel. A traditional measure of beer volume equal to 31 U.S. gallons. The most common containers of draft beer in the United States are half and quarter barrels, or kegs, at 15.5 gallons and 7.75 gallons, respectively, though the one-sixth-barrel kegs (about 5.2 gallons), known as sixtels, are becoming popular with microbrewers.

Beer. A fermented beverage brewed from grain, generally malted barley. "Beer" covers a variety of beverages, including ales and lagers, stouts and bocks, porters and pilsners, lambics and altbiers, cream ale, Kölsch, wheat beer, and a whole lot more.

Beer geek. A person who takes beer a little more seriously than does the average person. Lew Bryson has been chided for using the term "geek" here, but he hasn't found another one he likes, so our apologies to those who object. Often homebrewers, beer geeks love to argue with other beer geeks about what makes exceptional beers exceptional. That is, if they've been able to agree on which beers are exceptional in the first place. A beer geek is the kind of person who would buy a book about traveling to breweries . . . the kind of person who would read the glossary of a beer book. Hey, hi there!

BMC. "Bud, Miller, Coors." Shorthand—usually derogatory—for mainstream lagers like these three brands. This has been used by craft beer enthusiasts since before it was "craft beer."

Bottle-conditioned. A beer that has been bottled with an added dose of live yeast. This living yeast causes the beer to mature and change as it ages over periods of one to thirty years or more. It will also "eat" any oxygen that may have been sealed in at bottling and keep the beer from oxidizing, a staling process that leads to sherryish and "wet cardboard" aromas in beer. Bottle-conditioned beer qualifies as "real ale."

***Brettanomyces*, or brett.** A wild yeast that is generally considered undesirable in a brewhouse because of the "barnyard" aromas and sourness it can create. However, brewers of some types of beer—lambic, Flanders Red, and the singular Orval—intentionally allow *Brettanomyces* to ferment in their beer for just those reasons. Some American brewers have embraced brett, and a small but devoted group of drinkers have embraced those beers.

Brewer. One who brews beer for commercial sale.

Breweriana. Brewery and beer memorabilia, such as trays, coasters, neon signs, steins, mirrors, and so on, including the objects of desire of the beer can and bottle collectors. Most collectors do this for fun, a few do it for money (breweriana is starting to command some big prices; just check eBay), but the weird thing about this is the number of breweriana collectors who don't drink beer.

Brewhouse. The vessels used to mash the malt and grains and boil the wort. The malt and grains are mashed in a vessel called a mash tun. Brewhouse size is generally given in terms of the capacity of the brewkettle, where the wort is boiled. A brewery's annual capacity is a function of brewhouse size, fermentation, and aging tank capacity, and the length of the aging cycle for the brewery's beers.

Brewpub. A brewery that sells the majority of its output on draft, on the premises, or a tavern that brews its own beer.

CAMRA. The CAMpaign for Real Ale, a British beer drinkers' consumer group formed in the early 1970s by beer drinkers irate over the disappearance of cask-conditioned ale. They have been very vocal and successful in bringing this traditional drink back to a place of importance in the United Kingdom. CAMRA sets high standards for cask-conditioned ale, which only a few brewers in the United States match.

Carbonation. The fizzy effects of carbon dioxide (CO_2) in solution in a liquid such as beer. Carbonation can be accomplished artificially by injecting the beer with the gas or naturally by trapping the CO_2, which is a by-product of fermentation. There is no intrinsic qualitative difference between beers carbonated by these two methods. Brewer's choice, essentially. Low carbonation will allow a broader array of flavors to come through, whereas high carbonation can result in a perceived bitterness. Most American drinkers prefer a higher carbonation.

Cask. A keg designed to serve cask-conditioned ale by gravity feed or by handpump, not by gas pressure. These casks may be made of wood, but most are steel with special plumbing.

Cask-conditioned beer. An unfiltered beer that is put in a cask before it is completely ready to serve. The yeast still in the beer continues to work and ideally brings the beer to perfection at the point of sale, resulting in a beautifully fresh beer that has a "soft" natural carbonation and beautiful array of aromas. The flip side to achieving this supreme freshness is that as the beer is poured, air replaces it in the cask, and the beer will become sour within five days. Bars should sell the cask out before then or remove it from sale. If you are served sour cask-conditioned beer, send it back. Better yet, ask politely for a taste before ordering. Cask-conditioned beer is generally served at cellar temperature (55 to 60 degrees Fahrenheit) and is lightly carbonated. Cask-conditioned beers are almost always ales, but some American brewers are experimenting with cask-conditioned lager beers.

Cold-filtering. The practice of passing finished beer through progressively finer filters (usually cellulose or ceramic) to strip out microorganisms that can spoil the beer when it is stored. Brewers like Coors and Miller, and also some smaller brewers, use cold-filtering as an alternative to pasteurization (see below). Some beer geeks complain that this "strip-filtering" robs beers of their more subtle complexities and some of their body. We're not sure about that, but we do know that unfiltered beer right from the brewery tank almost always tastes more intense than the filtered, packaged beer.

Contract brewer. A brewer who hires an existing brewery to brew beer on contract. Contract brewers range from those who simply have a different label put on one of the brewery's existing brands to those who maintain a separate on-site staff to actually brew the beer at the brewery. Some brewers and beer geeks feel contract-brewed beer is inherently inferior. This is strictly a moral and business issue; some of the best beers on the market are contract-brewed.

Craft brewer. The new term for *microbrewer*. Craft brewer, like microbrewer before it, is really a code word for any brewer producing beers other than mainstream American lagers like Budweiser and Miller Lite.

Decoction. The type of mashing often used by lager brewers to wring the full character from the malt. In a decoction mash, a portion of the hot mash is taken to another vessel, brought to boiling, and returned to the mash, thus raising the temperature. See also *infusion*.

Draft. Beer dispensed from a tap, whether from a keg or a cask. Draft beer is not pasteurized, is kept under optimum conditions throughout the wholesaler-retailer chain, and is shockingly cheaper than bottled or canned beer (each half-barrel keg is more than seven cases of beer; check some prices and do the math). Kegs are available in 5-, 7.75-, and 15.5-gallon sizes, and almost all are now the straight-sided kegs with handles. Kegs are also ultimately recyclable, with a lifespan of forty years. Do what we do: Get draft beer for your next party.

Dry-hopping. Adding hops to the beer in postfermentation stages, often in porous bags to allow easy removal. This results in a greater hop aroma in the finished beer. A few brewers put a small bag of hop cones in each cask of their cask-conditioned beers, resulting in a particularly intense hop aroma in a glass of the draft beer.

ESB. Extra Special Bitter, an ale style with a rich malt character and full body, perhaps some butter or butterscotch aromas, and an understated hop bitterness. An ESB is, despite its name, not particularly bitter, especially compared with an American IPA.

Esters. Aroma compounds produced by fermentation that give some ales lightly fruity aromas: banana, pear, and grapefruit, among others. The aromas produced are tightly linked to the yeast strain used. Ester-based aromas should not be confused with the less subtle fruit aromas of a beer to which fruit or fruit essences have been added.

Fermentation. The miracle of yeast; the heart of making beer. Fermentation is the process in which yeast turns sugar and water into alcohol, heat, carbon dioxide, esters, and traces of other compounds.

Final gravity. See *gravity*.

Firkin. A cask or keg holding 9 gallons of beer, specially plumbed for gravity or handpump dispense.

GABF. See *Great American Beer Festival*.

Geekerie. The collective of beer geeks, particularly the beer-oriented, beer-fascinated, beer-above-all beer geeks. The geekerie sometimes can fall victim to group thinking and a herd mentality, but they are generally good people, if a bit hop-headed and malt-maniacal. If you're not a member of the geekerie, you might want to consider getting to know them: They usually know where all the best bars and beer stores are in their town, and they're more than happy to share the knowledge and even go along with you to share the fun. All you have to do is ask. See the Beerwebs section for links to the better beer pages, a good way to hook up with them.

Gravity. The specific gravity of wort (original gravity) or finished beer (terminal gravity). The ratio of dissolved sugars to water determines the gravity of the wort. If there are more dissolved sugars, the original gravity and the potential alcohol are higher. The sugar that is converted to alcohol by the yeast lowers the terminal gravity and makes the beer drier, just like wine. A brewer can determine the alcohol content of a beer by mathematical comparison of its original gravity and terminal gravity.

Great American Beer Festival (GABF). Since 1982, America's breweries have been invited each year to bring their best beer to the GABF in Denver to showcase what America can brew. Since 1987, the GABF has awarded medals for various styles of beer. To ensure impartiality, the beers are tasted blind, their identities hidden from the judges. GABF medals are the most prestigious awards in American brewing because of the festival's longevity and reputation for fairness.

Growler. A jug or bottle used to take home draft beer. These are usually either simple half-gallon glass jugs with screwtops or more elaborate molded glass containers with swingtop seals. Lew Bryson has traced the origin of the term *growler* back to a cheap, four-wheeled horse cab in use in Victorian London. These cabs would travel a circuit of pubs in the evenings, and riding from pub to pub was known as "working the growler." To bring a pail of beer home to have with dinner was to anticipate the night's work of drinking and became known as "rushing the growler." When the growler cabs disappeared from the scene, we were left with only the phrase, and "rushing the growler" was assumed to mean hurrying home with the bucket. When Ed Otto revived the practice by selling jugs of Otto Brothers beer at his Jackson Hole brewery in the mid-1980s, he called them growlers. Now you know where the term really came from.

Guest taps/guest beers. Beers made by other brewers that are offered at brewpubs.

Handpump. A hand-powered pump for dispensing beer from a keg, also called a beer engine. Either a handpump or a gravity tap (putting the barrel on the bar and pounding in a simple spigot) is always used for dispensing cask-conditioned beer; however, the presence of a handpump does not guarantee that the beer being dispensed is cask-conditioned.

Homebrewing. Making honest-to-goodness beer at home for personal consumption. Homebrewing is where many American craft brewers got their start.

Hops. The spice of beer. Hop plants (*Humulus lupus*) are vines whose flowers have a remarkable effect on beer. The flowers' resins and oils add bitterness and a variety of aromas (spicy, piney, citrusy, and others) to the finished beer. Beer without hops would be more like a fizzy, sweet "alco-soda."

IBU. International Bittering Unit, a measure of a beer's bitterness. Humans can first perceive bitterness at levels between 8 and 12 IBU. Budweiser has 11.5 IBU, Heineken 18, Sierra Nevada Pale Ale 32, Pilsner Urquell 43, and a monster like Sierra Nevada Bigfoot clocks in at 98 IBU. Equivalent amounts of bitterness will seem greater in a lighter-bodied beer, whereas a heavier, maltier beer like Bigfoot needs lots of bitterness to be perceived as balanced.

Imperial. A beer-style intensifier, indicating a beer that is hoppier and stronger. Once there was an imperial court in St. Petersburg, Russia, the court of the czars. It supported a trade with England in strong, heavy, black beers, massive versions of the popular English porters, which became known as imperial porters and somewhat later as imperial stouts. Then in the late 1990s, American brewers started brewing IPAs with even more hops than the ridiculous amounts they were already using, at a gravity that led to beers of 7.5 percent ABV and up. What to call them? They looked at the imperial stouts and grabbed the apparent intensifier: "Imperial" IPA was born. While this is still the most common usage, this shorthand for "hoppier and stronger" has been applied to a variety of types, including pilsner and—amusingly—porter.

Infusion. The mashing method generally used by ale brewers. Infusion entails heating the mash in a single vessel until the starches have been converted to sugar. There is single infusion, in which the crushed malt (grist) is mixed with hot water and steeped without further heating, and step infusion, in which the mash is held for short periods at rising temperature points. Infusion mashing is simpler than decoction mashing and works well with most types of modern malt.

IPA. India Pale Ale, a British ale style that has been almost completely co-opted by American brewers, characterized in this country by intense hops bitterness, accompanied in better examples of the style by a full-malt body. The name derives from the style's origin as a beer brewed for export to British beer drinkers in India. The beer was strong and heavily laced with hops—a natural preservative—to better endure the long sea voyage. Some British brewers claim that the beer was brewed that way in order to be diluted upon arrival in India, a kind of "beer concentrate" that saved on shipping costs.

Kräusening. The practice of carbonating beer by a second fermentation. After the main fermentation has taken place and its vigorous blowoff of carbon dioxide has been allowed to escape, a small amount of fresh wort is added to the tank. A second fermentation takes place, and the carbon dioxide is captured in solution. General opinion is that there is little sensory difference between kräusened beer and beer carbonated by injection, but some brewers use this more traditional method.

Lager. The generic term for all cold-fermented beers. Lager has also been appropriated as a name for the lightly hopped pilsners that have become the world's most popular beers, such as Budweiser, Ki-Rin, Brahma, Heineken, and Foster's. Many people speak of pilsners and lagers as if they are two different syles of beer, which is incorrect. All pilsners are lagers, but not all lagers are pilsners. Some are bocks, hellesbiers, and Märzens.

Lambic. A very odd style of beer brewed in Belgium that could take pages to explain. Suffice it to say that the beer is fermented spontaneously by airborne wild yeasts and bacteria that are resident in the aged wooden fermenting casks. The beer's sensory characteristics have been described as funky, barnyard, and horseblanket . . . it's an acquired taste. But once you have that taste, lambics can be extremely rewarding. Most knowledgeable people believe that the beers can be brewed only in a small area of Belgium, because of the peculiarities of the wild yeasts. But some American brewers have had a degree of success in replicating this character by carefully using prepared cultures of yeasts and bacteria.

Malt. Generally this refers to malted barley, although other grains can be malted and used in brewing. Barley is wetted and allowed to sprout, which causes the hard, stable starches in the grain to convert to soluble starches (and small amounts of sugars). The grains, now called malt, are kiln-dried to kill the sprouts and conserve the starches. Malt is responsible for the color of beer. The kilned malt can be roasted, which will darken its color and intensify its flavors like a French roast coffee.

Mash. A mixture of cracked grains of malt and water, which is then heated. Heating causes starches in the malt to convert to sugars, which will be consumed by the yeast in fermentation. The length of time the mash is heated, temperatures, and techniques used are crucial to the character of the finished beer. Two mashing techniques are infusion and decoction.

Megabrewer. A mainstream brewer, generally producing 5 million or more barrels of American-style pilsner beer annually. Anheuser-Busch, Miller, and Coors are the best-known megabrewers.

Microbrewer. A somewhat dated term, originally defined as a brewer producing less than 15,000 barrels of beer in a year. Microbrewer, like craft brewer, is generally applied to any brewer producing beers other than mainstream American lagers.

Original gravity. See *gravity.*

Pasteurization. A process named for its inventor, Louis Pasteur, the famed French microbiologist. Pasteurization involves heating beer to kill the microorganisms in it. This keeps beer fresh longer, but unfortunately it also changes the flavor, because the beer is essentially cooked. "Flash pasteurization" sends fresh beer through a heated pipe where most of the microorganisms are killed; here the beer is hot for only twenty seconds or so, as opposed to the twenty to thirty minutes of regular "tunnel" pasteurization. See also *cold-filtering.*

Pilsner. The Beer That Conquered the World. Developed in 1842 in Pilsen (now Plzen, in the Czech Republic), it is a hoppy pale lager that quickly became known as pilsner or pilsener, a German word meaning simply "from Pilsen." Pilsner rapidly became the most popular beer in the world and now accounts for more than 80 percent of all beer consumed worldwide. Budweiser, a less hoppy, more delicate version of pilsner, was developed in the Czech town of Budejovice, formerly known as Budweis. Anheuser-Busch's Budweiser, the world's best-selling beer, is quite a different animal.

Pitching. The technical term for adding yeast to wort.

Prohibition. The period from 1920 to 1933 when the sale, manufacture, or transportation of alcoholic beverages was illegal in the United States, thanks to the Eighteenth Amendment and the Volstead Act. Prohibition had a disastrous effect on American brewing and brought about a huge growth in organized crime and government corruption. Repeal of Prohibition came with ratification of the Twenty-first Amendment in December 1933. Beer drinkers, however, had gotten an eight-month head start when the Volstead Act, the enforcement legislation of Prohibition, was amended to allow sales of 3.2 percent ABW beer. The amendment took effect at midnight, April 7. According to Will Anderson's *From Beer to Eternity*, more than 1 million barrels of beer were consumed on April 7: 2,323,000 six-packs each hour.

Real ale. See *cask-conditioned beer.*

Regional brewery. Somewhere between a micro- and a megabrewer. Annual production by regional breweries ranges from 35,000 to 2 million barrels. They generally brew mainstream American lagers.

However, some microbrewers—Boston Beer Company, New Belgium, and Sierra Nevada, for instance—have climbed to this production level, and some regional brewers, such as Anchor, Matt's, and August Schell, have reinvented themselves and now produce craft-brewed beer.

Reinheitsgebot. The German beer purity law, which has its roots in a 1516 Bavarian statute limiting the ingredients in beer to barley malt, hops, and water. The law evolved into an inch-thick book and was the cornerstone of high-quality German brewing. It was deemed anticompetitive by the European Community courts and overturned in 1988. Most German brewers, however, continue to brew by its standards; tradition and the demands of their customers ensure it.

Repeal. See *Prohibition*.

Session beer. A beer that is low to medium-low in strength, say 3 to 4.5 percent ABV, but still flavorful, designed for what the British call "session drinking," the kind that goes on all evening through tons of talk and maybe some snacks, and doesn't leave you knee-wobbling after four pints.

Sixtel. A new size of keg developed in 1996, holding one-sixth of a barrel: 5.2 gallons, or about 2.5 cases. Very popular for home use, and popular with multitaps as well. The beer stays fresher, and you can fit more different beers in a cold box. The word sixtel is of uncertain origin; it was not coined by the developer of the keg but apparently grew up among the users.

Swill. A derogatory term used by beer geeks for American mainstream beers. The beers do not really deserve the name, since they are made with pure ingredients under conditions of quality control and sanitation some micros only wish they could achieve.

Terminal gravity. See *gravity*.

Three-tier system. A holdover from before Prohibition, the three-tier system requires brewers, wholesalers, and retailers to be separate entities. The system was put in place to curtail financial abuses that were common when the three were mingled. Owning both wholesale and retail outlets gave unscrupulous brewers the power to rake off huge amounts of money, which all too often was used to finance political graft and police corruption. The three-tier system keeps the wholesaler insulated from pressure from the brewer and puts a layer of separation between brewer and retailer. Recent court rulings have put the future of the regulated three-tier system in serious doubt, which may spell paradise or disaster for beer drinkers.

Wort. The prebeer grain broth of sugars, proteins, hop oils, alpha acids, and whatever else was added or developed during the mashing process. Once the yeast has been pitched and starts its jolly work, wort becomes beer.

Yeast. A miraculous fungus that, among other things, converts sugar into alcohol and carbon dioxide. The particular yeast strain used in brewing beer greatly influences the aroma and flavor of the beer. An Anheuser-Busch brewmaster once told Lew that the yeast strain used there is the major factor in the flavor and aroma of Budweiser. Yeast is the sole source of the clovey, banana-rama aroma and the taste of Bavarian-style wheat beers. The original Reinheitsgebot of 1516 made no mention of yeast; it hadn't been discovered yet. Early brewing depended on a variety of sources for yeast: adding a starter from the previous batch of beer; exposing the wort to the wild yeasts carried on the open air (a method still used for Belgian lambic beers); always using the same vats for fermentation (yeast would cling to cracks and pores in the wood); or stirring the beer with a "magic stick" (which had the dormant yeast from the last batch dried on its surface). British brewers called the turbulent, billowing foam on fermenting beer goddesgood—"God is good"— because the foam meant that the predictable magic of the yeast was making beer. Amen.

Zwickel. A *zwickel* ("tzVICK-el") is a little spout coming off the side of a beer tank that allows the brewer to sample the maturing beer in small amounts; it is also sometimes called a "pigtail." If you're lucky, your tour will include an unfiltered sample of beer tapped directly from the tank through this little spout. Some brewers are touchy about this, as the zwickel is a potential site for infection, but with proper care, it's perfectly harmless to "tickle the zwickel." It's delicious, too: Unfiltered beer is the hot ticket.

Index